Fourth Edition

Writing History

A Guide for Canadian Students

William Kelleher Storey & Towser Jones

OXFORD
UNIVERSITY PRESS

Oxford University Press is a department of the University of Oxford.
It furthers the University's objective of excellence in research, scholarship,
and education by publishing worldwide. Oxford is a registered trade mark of
Oxford University Press in the UK and in certain other countries.

Published in Canada by
Oxford University Press
8 Sampson Mews, Suite 204,
Don Mills, Ontario M3C 0H5 Canada

www.oupcanada.com

Library and Archives Canada Cataloguing in Publication

Storey, William Kelleher, author
Writing history : a guide for Canadian students / William
Kelleher Storey, Towser Jones. – Fourth edition.

Includes bibliographical references and index.
ISBN 978-0-19-901212-1 (paperback)

1. History—Research. 2. History—Research—Canada.
3. Academic writing. 4. Historiography. I. Jones, Towser, author
II. Title.

D16.S76 2016   907.2   C2015-906406-6

Cover image: Kevin Clogstoun/Getty Images

Oxford University Press is committed to our environment.
Wherever possible, our books are printed on paper which comes from
responsible sources.

Printed and bound in The United States of America

1 2 3 4 — 19 18 17 16

Contents

Preface to the Fourth Canadian Edition

William Kelleher Storey's book *Writing History* had its origins in the Harvard Writing Project and was first published by Oxford University Press in 1999. Following the success of his second edition, Oxford asked me to write a Canadian adaptation (2003; revised 2008 and 2011).

Why would we need a fourth Canadian edition of this text? It is still true that while Canadians are accustomed to reading books from elsewhere and to seeing Canada as part of a global culture, the Canadian context and many aspects of the Canadian experience are unique. These can be looked at through the lens of Canadian historians and their work not only in Canadian history but also in other areas of the discipline. Historians' lenses constantly shift focus, and the fourth edition will recognize some of the new work that historians are producing. It is also important to recognize how the needs of students continue to change.

Preparing this fourth edition has been both a pleasure and a challenge. Though I've continued to preserve Storey's informal tone and practical approach, the text has been extensively reorganized and updated, with expanded coverage of electronic resources and Canadian research materials, as well as additional examples that should have particular meaning to Canadian students, whether they relate specifically to Canadian history or to other areas. There are many excellent Canadian historians, and I hope this edition will serve as an introduction to at least a few of them and to the impressive variety of their work.

As always, I am delighted to honour my many debts. Tamara Capar at Oxford was a pleasure to work with, supportive and enormously helpful. Copy editor Heather Macdougall, who was both kind and thorough, saved me from a variety of errors. Several anonymous reviewers offered useful advice, much of which I followed. Any errors that remain, of course, are not their fault. Capilano University provided a leave to allow me time to complete this project. My friends and colleagues in the History Department, Nanci Lucas and Denis Dubord, offered encouragement and ideas. Reference librarian Trevor Smith explained some of the complexities of the modern academic library. I am also very grateful to my former students Justin Elsworth and Alice Gorton, who generously allowed me to use extracts from their papers as examples. Finally, and as always, my most profound thanks go to my family, Don, Katriona, Max, and Jake.

Introduction

What is history? No single definition is universally accepted, but historians do generally agree on several points. History is not a compilation of names and dates to be memorized and regurgitated. Nor is it the simple description of "what happened" in the past. History is not a matter of right and wrong answers. It reflects the time in which it is written. It demands critical analysis, questioning and exploration, selection, debate, and interpretation.

Historians study the human past, ancient and recent, to understand not only what happened, but how and why, what it means and why it matters. And it does matter. Understanding the past gives us a basis for understanding the present. In the words of the Canadian historian Margaret MacMillan, "History is not a dead subject. . . .[It] lies under the present, silently shaping our institutions, our ways of thought, our likes and dislikes."[1] Historians seek to understand the significance of past events and people not only in their own times, but also in the present. Not surprisingly, historians frequently disagree with one another. Thus Louis Riel has been seen as a villain and a hero, a champion of Aboriginal and of Francophone rights, a misunderstood genius and a lunatic. Such debates are so common that there is a whole subfield of the discipline called **historiography**, the study of writing history—in a sense, the history of history.

Writing history is about making decisions. First, historians choose the subjects they think are most important. Then they choose the source materials they judge most likely to shed useful light on those subjects. After carefully analyzing all the evidence they can find, they develop arguments and draw conclusions in the light of that evidence. Finally, they choose how they will present their arguments in writing so as to balance respect for their subjects with the needs of their readers.

The best historians are so skilled at making choices that they can transform painstaking research into seamless arguments and narratives. But don't be fooled. The process of writing is filled with difficult decisions. Even with the best sources and methods, writing history can be like trying to "nail jelly to a wall."[2] For this reason, historians experiment with many approaches to the past, although in the end they must choose an approach that suits their subject.

Selection has been central to Western historical writing ever since the time of the ancient Greeks. When the Athenian general Thucydides composed his history of the Peloponnesian Wars, around 400 BCE, he could hardly report everything that had taken place over 30 years of battles and defeats. Instead, he chose to focus on decisive moments. Among the latter was the famous eulogy for the Athenian dead delivered by the statesman and general Pericles:

> I have no wish to make a long speech on subjects familiar to you all: so I shall say nothing about the warlike deeds by which we acquired our power or the battles in which we or our fathers gallantly resisted our enemies, Greek or foreign. What I want to do is, in the first place, to discuss the spirit in which we faced our trials and also our constitution and the way of life which has made us great. After that I shall speak in praise of the dead. . .[3]

Thucydides chose to make Pericles' speech a part of his history not just because he found it moving, but because he believed it to be instructive on the nature of Athenian democracy.

Like Thucydides, modern-day historians also tend to choose subjects that they believe to be relevant to contemporary circumstances. In response to a recent debate on the value of teaching Canadian history, for instance, Ruth Sandwell, a specialist in the history of education, edited a collection of essays exploring "history education, public memory, and citizenship in Canada." Sandwell and her contributors linked their concerns about the current teaching of history in Canadian schools to "some of the deeper problems that we, as a society, have about how knowledge, identity and power are created and sustained within our social system."[4]

Like Thucydides, historians also choose subjects that they believe can shed light on the causes of change over time. To that end, they must learn how to find sources, how to report on them faithfully, and how to use them to make inferences about the past.

Approaches to historical research vary widely. If you go into a library and browse through any shelf of history books, you will see that even historians who work in the same narrow geographical and chronological specialties approach their subjects from many different perspectives. They incorporate methods and insights not only from other historians but from scholars in the humanities, the natural sciences, and the social sciences as well. Thus Arthur Ray, in *I Have Lived Here Since the World Began*, draws on geography, literature, anthropology, and economics to recount the history of Canada's First Nations.[5] In fact, the variety of angles from which historians approach their subjects is almost endless. Despite the diversity of their approaches, however, all historians share a commitment to accurate reporting, persuasive argument, and clear communication—in short, to good writing. *Writing History* is designed to introduce undergraduate historians in Canada to the discipline and its challenges. We use examples from Canadian history and from Canadian historians' work in a variety of time periods and geographical areas. Thus we intend that *Writing History* will be useful for all undergraduate history students, no matter what are the focuses of their specific courses. Chapter 1 of the fourth edition offers a brief guide to various history writing assignments, including an expanded discussion of oral history projects, as well as some hints to help with history exams. This guide is followed by a discussion of the classic research paper. We then use the research paper as an illustration to guide students through the preparation and writing process that is the basis of almost all history assignments. Chapter by chapter, *Writing History* explains the processes of planning, finding a topic, researching, analyzing and incorporating sources, building arguments, and creating a finished work. In addition, the fourth edition has been extensively revised to enhance its practical value for students and instructors alike. Among its new features are appendices on referencing methodology and online resources for history students. We have also added Tip boxes throughout the text to provide handy hints and reminders of important points. We have retained the essay concept map charting all the stages of the research and writing process, designed to help visual learners in particular. While the complete map can be found in Appendix A at the end of the book, the relevant portions are repeated at the ends of Chapters 2–4, 6, and 10, to facilitate review of the chapter material. Students will be able to check the map in the appendix as they work through the researching and writing process to ensure that they have not missed any steps and to keep visual track of their progress.

Key terms are bolded at first use and clearly defined in a glossary at the end of the book, while boxes at the end of each chapter highlight its key points. A handy Reference Guide inside the front cover tells readers where they can find answers to many frequently asked questions. Finally, inside the back cover are three checklists that students can use to make sure they have covered all the bases before submitting a paper.

Understanding History Assignments

This book is concerned with helping you to prepare and write the most frequently assigned projects in post-secondary history courses. Instructors assign many types of projects. The specifics vary, but most of the assignments rely on the same basic techniques that are discussed in detail throughout this book: library research, checking and analysis of sources, careful documentation, and the creation of thoughtful and persuasive **arguments**. No matter what the assignment, always pay close attention to your instructor's specific requirements and instructions, document your work carefully, and keep all your notes and **drafts**. In this chapter, we will discuss some commonly assigned history projects. At the end of the chapter and over the following chapters, we will use the classic history assignment, a historical research paper, as a vehicle to illustrate the process of assignment preparation.

Book and Article Reviews

History students are frequently asked to review books or articles. Whatever form the material takes, your job is to summarize and assess it.

Book Review

Historians frequently consult book reviews to find new work relevant to their area of study. Learning to write a useful review requires practice. A book review assignment allows you to gain this practice as well as to become familiar with a specific subject and to hone your analytical skills. It goes beyond the scope of a book report, which is essentially an extended summary, to look at the book's theme and purpose, its evidence and arguments, and its conclusions and significance. If you have never written a book review, you may find it helpful to look at examples in scholarly journals such as the *Canadian Historical Review* or the *Canadian Journal of History.*

The first step is obvious: read the book. There is no substitute for careful and thoughtful reading of the entire work, although it is definitely useful to scan the introduction, chapter headings, and conclusion up front. As you read, note the author's main points and your observations of the evidence or arguments, as well as any short passages that you may want to quote in your review.

Once you have read the book, you can plan your approach. Does the assignment require you to look at other sources so as to put the book into a wider context? Are you supposed to link this book to the themes or materials of your course, or simply to review it according to your own evaluation of its merits? If you do further reading, pay attention to matters relating to "your" book's main arguments and evidence, especially if other sources emphasize significant ideas or events that your book seems to skim over or ignore. Don't let yourself get sidetracked by details that are insignificant or unrelated to the book's main arguments. Also think about the criteria you will use to evaluate it. Your personal response to the book—what you liked or didn't like about it—is not irrelevant, but your responsibility as a reviewer is to judge the strength of its arguments and evidence, identify its strengths and weaknesses, and assess its usefulness. If you have some knowledge of the subject from other sources, you can think about how this book fits in: does it generally agree, disagree, offer a new perspective? If you are evaluating the book on its own merits, try to place it in the context of the themes and materials you are studying in your course.

When your reading and research are complete and you have decided on the main points to discuss, you are ready to begin writing. Be sure to follow your instructor's guidelines regarding length and presentation. Typically, a review will begin with a bibliographical reference that lists the author, title, and publication information for the work under review. Unless you have been instructed otherwise, summarize the work briefly, being careful to focus on the main points and the relevant evidence. Include a thesis statement that makes your overall opinion of the book clear. This would also be a good place to mention the author's background and qualifications: whether he or she is a professional historian, has specific expertise in the area, or has written other books on this or related subjects. You could also mention the arrangement of the book's contents, any additional features such as illustrations, and the style of writing. Keep these details brief, though; you want as much space as possible for substantive discussion of the book's contents.

The body of the review will present your assessment of the book's arguments, evidence, and conclusion. Consider whether the author has achieved his or her goal and whether you are convinced by the arguments. You may include some quotations from the book, as long as they are short, relevant to your point, and representative of the book's contents, tone, and ideas. Just be sure not to take any quotation out of context—otherwise you run the risk of misrepresenting the author's meaning—and never quote anything just for the sake of quoting.

The last component of any book review is the conclusion. In this paragraph, summarize your main points, give your overall assessment of the book, and (if appropriate to the assignment) make a recommendation to your reader.

Throughout the writing process, remember that your job is to give your readers a clear, balanced idea of the book as a whole. Don't focus on one area of the work while ignoring other equally significant areas. And don't feel that you have to find something negative to say in order to fulfill your role as a critic. No book is perfect, and it's perfectly legitimate to note flaws if you find them, but you should be equally ready to praise the book's strengths. Finally, be sure to back up both your praise and your criticism with specific examples.

Comparative Book Review

A second type of book review assignment requires you to compare two or three different books. If your professor leaves the selection of works to you, look for books on topics that bear some relationship to one another. Once you have found some likely candidates, take a quick look through them to be sure there is a real basis for comparison. Two biographies of Louis Riel would obviously work well for this type of essay. But one on Riel himself and one on Canadian federal policy towards First Nations peoples in the nineteenth century might also allow you to make some useful commentary. Writing a coherent comparison of a book on Riel and a book on women in the fur trade would be a much tougher job.

Once you have selected your books, go through them and note any points of similarity or difference, agreement or disagreement. Are there any areas where one book sheds light on the other? When you have finished your careful reading you can decide which points are significant and which can be ignored. For example, suppose you were reviewing Reinhold Kramer's scholarly biography *Mordecai Richler: Leaving St. Urbain* in tandem with Joe King's **popular history** *From the Ghetto to the Main: The Story of Jews in Montreal*. King's portrait of the novelist's home community—which he fled as a young man and returned to in middle age—might give you some additional insight into the Richler portrayed by Kramer, who places his subject in the context of a changing Jewish culture in Montreal and the world. A comparative review of King and Kramer might also allow you to comment on the differences between **popular** and **scholarly history**, that is, history written for a scholarly audience and history written for the general public.[6] Of course you won't be able to discuss everything the two authors say: just pick out the most significant areas. Now you can consider how to organize your review.

Start as before, with full bibliographical references, an introduction, and a short description of each book. Now there are two ways to proceed: you can discuss each book in its own section and then compare some of their points, or you can organize your paper thematically and compare the books directly, point by point. One way to choose between these approaches is to consider how directly the two works can be compared. If you have books with related but not identical subjects, can you find more than one or two significant elements to compare directly? If not, it might be easier to go with option number one. If you can find significant points that are directly comparable, then you might choose option number two.

Article Review

A third very common review assignment concentrates on one or more articles as opposed to books. The overall task is the same, but you will most likely be given fewer pages to work with. In this case it is crucial to keep your summary of the articles short so that you have adequate space for analytical comments.

> **TIP!** You can use the same techniques to review movie or television programs, or even websites.

Historiographical Paper

Historiography is the study of how history is written—in effect, how historians shape history through their work. Thus a historiography paper generally takes a topic that has generated continuing interest and explores how historians have written about it.

History is not static. Interpretations of the past change because, as John H. Arnold points out, "History is above all else an argument. It is an argument between different historians; and, perhaps, an argument between the past and present."[7]

Historians do not generally strive for "the right answer." They strive to interpret the available evidence as fully and accurately as they can. Even when working with exactly the same evidence, their opinions frequently differ. Thus when Robin Fisher's re-examination of sources led him to portray the indigenous peoples of the Pacific coast as savvy traders who were fully capable of holding their own against Europeans, he challenged the standard interpretation and stimulated a flurry of new interest and new opinions on the subject. In other words, he started an argument, in the best intellectual sense of the term—which is exactly what new research ought to do.

Historians' interests and approaches also reflect their own times and circumstances. In the 1960s and 1970s, historians responded to the growth of feminist activism with a new interest in the history of women as a separate topic from the history of men. More recently, with the discussion of gay rights in Canada, interest in queer history has increased. Recent years have also seen growing interest in local history, the history of childhood, and environmental history.

What kinds of subjects might be suitable for a historiographical paper? You could look at the historiography of a theme such as the development of the Canadian labour movement, an event such as the Oka Crisis of 1990, or a person such as Louis Riel or Prime Minister Mackenzie King. Any topic that has been controversial or that historians have revisited in different ways over time would be suitable. It is also possible to write a historiographical paper about a particular historian, tracing the development of his or her work.

Typically, a historiographical paper will focus on how historians' approaches, themes, and questions have developed over the years and from place to place, providing insight into the historians and their times as well as the historical topic under discussion. Look for continuing or recurring themes, new themes and reassessments of old themes, and agreements and disagreements. The point is not particularly to review or critique the works or historians in question, although you could well include some comments along these lines. Rather, the point is to examine change over time, to explore how and why historians' methods, interests, and approaches have changed. You might also consider the direction in which the historiography of your topic is likely to develop in the future. For instance, if your paper is focused on the historiography of the energy industry in Canada, considering recent debates on oil and gas pipelines, you might speculate that environmental historians will soon be paying a lot of attention to this topic. A chronological organization usually works well for historiographical papers, but you could modify this format to discuss sub-themes such as the influence of gender or ethnicity on the writing of history.

Primary Document Analysis

Primary sources are not limited to documents. They can include any sort of physical object from the era under study, from burial sites and gravestones to household items and coins to photographs and works of art. Although all of these are well worth studying, in this section we will focus on documents. Among the primary documents that professional historians rely on are letters, diaries, newspaper accounts, government documents, legal papers, tax statements, and church records, to name only a few. Instructors often set document analysis assignments to give students an opportunity to conduct primary research and get a stronger feel for the times under study than **secondary sources** can give. Primary documents can be tricky to read if they are written in archaic or extremely formal language. Have a good dictionary close by and use it to look up anything you don't understand. If the document is very old, you may need to consult the full-length *Oxford English Dictionary* (as opposed to the various shorter and "concise" editions), which gives the history of a word's usage as well as current meanings. The complete OED runs to 20 volumes, so you will need to find it in a library or (by subscription) online.

Primary document analysis demands that you bring your critical abilities to bear. All historical documents, public as well as private, were produced by real people who were influenced by the times and places in which they lived, as well as by their own experiences. This means that you need to keep the context in mind as you read. Your instructor will not simply be looking for a summary of what the document says, but rather a thoughtful analysis of what it means and what it can tell us about people, places, and events. The simplest way to approach document analysis is to follow the "question" model outlined below and in more detail in Chapter 3. You won't always be able to answer every question suggested here, and sometimes the answers—the whys and hows, or the wheres and whens—will overlap. Still, posing the questions will help you to think carefully about your document.

The "who" question. Who wrote the document? What do you know (or what can you find out) about the author(s)? How does this person's background or experience help to explain his or her point of view? Was the author personally involved in, or affected by, the events discussed in the document? Looking at it from the other side, what does the document tell you about its author? What can you say about his or her values or outlook on the basis of the document?

The "what" question. What is this document? Is it official (say, a government report) or private (a diary entry)? What can you learn from it about the time and place in which it was written?

The "why" question. Why was this document written? Was it intended to influence others, or to express a personal point of view? Did the author want to influence events or opinions to come, or to explain events that had already occurred?

The "when" question. When was the document written? Was it contemporary to the events it discusses or describes? If not, was it written before or after the events? Does this chronological relationship make a difference to your understanding of the document? To your assessment of its value or validity?

The "how" question. How was this document produced? How was it supposed to be used? How was it actually used? How was it preserved, and does that make a difference to your assessment of the document?

Oral History Project

Traditionally, historians have relied on written sources, but in recent decades they have become increasingly aware of the limits that this approach imposes. Before reasonably modern times, for example, most people were unable to read or write, and therefore they could not leave written accounts of their existence or experience. Written records thus reflected the interests and views of the literate minority, politicians and those in power, and the voices of the majority were for the most part either ignored or viewed through the eyes of the powerful and educated. In addition, there are many peoples (Canada's Aboriginal peoples among them) whose histories have been transmitted orally rather than in writing. Oral history techniques have provided essential insights into people whose lives and experiences otherwise might be lost to history. Oral history is a subfield of history and it has its own guidelines, both practical and ethical. You can find handbooks and guides from around the world on the Canadian Oral History Association's website at oralhistorycentre. ca. One very useful starting point included on this site is UCLA Berkeley's "The One-Minute Guide to Conducting Oral History." For considerably more detailed and wide-ranging information and guidelines, also see the website of the American Oral History Association.

Interviewing people is one of the most exciting aspects of historical research, and personal interviews can give fascinating insight into some topic areas. Be sure to choose your interview subject carefully. Does he or she have personal knowledge or expertise in the topic you want to explore? For instance, if you were planning a paper on Canadian forces in the Korean War, perhaps you could interview a veteran from the Princess Patricia's Canadian Light Infantry, which arrived in Korea in the early 1950s. If you know a doctor who specializes in the treatment of stress disorders, he or she might be able to give you some valuable insights into the post-traumatic stress suffered by many soldiers. If you find it difficult to ask someone for an interview, keep in mind that most people will be flattered to know that their life or work is historically significant. But an interview is more than just a conversation: it's a way to seek critical information about the past. Therefore you should be as systematic as possible in your interviewing. Here are some initial guidelines:

1. **Do your homework.** Before you conduct the interview, learn all that you can from written sources. Then make a list of historically significant questions that you want to ask your subject. Try to make sure that you have all the background information you need, and that you have a clear idea of what you want to find out. Otherwise, you will simply waste your subject's time as well your own. This doesn't mean that you should close off all avenues of discussion except those that you have determined in advance—in fact it is important to allow your subject to give his or her testimony in his or her own way. It does mean that your work should have a point to it, and that this point should be clear both to you and to your subject. Otherwise, your subject may think that you don't know what you're talking about and may not trust you enough to give you much useful information. If you think that the subject is digressing too far or straying into material that is not particularly relevant to your project or intentions you can gently draw them back, but be careful to show respect: this is their interview as well as yours.

2. **Be sure to understand the legalities.** If you are a student, find out from your instructor whether your college or university has published ethical guidelines for conducting research on human subjects. If this is the case, be sure to follow the guidelines. Graduate students, postdoctoral researchers, and faculty members will almost certainly be obliged to follow the university's standards for research on human subjects, and as far as possible you should too. You can find Canadian guidelines on the Oral History Association's website (see page 8). You will probably need to obtain a signed release from your interview subjects indicating that they understand the terms of the interview arrangement and are willing to have their testimony used in the way you intend (see Figure 1.1 for an example of a release form). You must be clear about your intentions. For example, are you planning to quote the interview in your paper or simply to refer to it? What will happen to the interview material once your own project is complete? Will you return all copies to your subject? Will you deposit them in your university's archives? Will you post them on any digital media? Your release form should be very clear about these issues. Be sure to tell your subjects beforehand about the goals and objectives of your project and about the release form, but do not ask them to sign it until the interviews are complete and they know what they are signing for.

3. **Be considerate.** Pay attention to what your subjects tell you, if only through their body language. If they seem uncomfortable, try to figure out why. Then do whatever is necessary to accommodate them. For instance, if they don't want to be identified, *you must respect their wishes.* Perhaps they would allow you to identify them by code names or numbers.

It's important to be honest when you are writing up an interview, but the feelings of the people involved are at least equally important and their legal protection is vital. Never repeat hurtful material if it is not necessary or if it would compromise someone who is not involved with the interview. For example, if an interview subject is discussing some indiscretion or illegal activity in his youth and tells you the name of someone else who was involved, you should probably not repeat that name in your paper. Even in the case of your subject, if he is saying something that could expose him, for example, to legal action, make sure that he is aware of it so that he can pull back if necessary. If in doubt, consult your instructor before proceeding.

Remember also that your schedule is not important to your interview subjects; be prepared to conduct the interviews at a time that suits them and in the place of their choice. People may prefer to do interviews in their homes, and this often is the best place, since you want them to be relaxed and open. In any case, do try to arrange for a quiet place where you won't be interrupted or distracted.

4. **Be patient.** It takes time to set up an interview, and you may have difficulty getting in touch with some subjects. It's often a good idea to have your personal references on hand to offer potential subjects, or even to mail them in advance a resumé and a brief description of your project. It may take two or three interviews before your subject trusts you enough to share interesting information with you. If you plan to interview people, start work on the project as soon as possible: that way you will have plenty of time to meet your deadlines.

5. **Take scrupulous notes.** Always take written notes during an interview. You may also want to use a tape or digital recorder, or even a camera, but outside noise can interfere, batteries can die, and the wrong buttons can get pressed. Back up your work with written notes. A recording device can also make a subject uncomfortable. If you notice that the device is interfering with the interview, turn it off and rely on your written notes. After you have completed each interview, transcribe the notes and give a copy to the subject. Also remember to send a note of thanks to every subject, as well as anyone who may have helped to set up the interviews.

TIP! Get working early on oral history projects!

ANYPLACE UNIVERSITY

Two copies of this form are required.
One signed copy of the form is to remain with the interview subject.
A second signed copy must be submitted to the course instructor.

Student Interviewer and contact information _____

Course for which the interviews are taking place _____

Course instructor and contact information _____

Participant _____

I agree to be interviewed by_____ as part of his/her research for _____ (course) at Anyplace University. I understand that the information from the taped/transcribed interview will be used as part of the research material for _____'s paper in _____ course at Anyplace University. I do ☐ /do not ☐ give my permission for one copy of any tapes, transcripts or photographs made during this project to be deposited in the library or archives of Anyplace University and used by undergraduate ☐ , graduate ☐ , and faculty researchers ☐, and the public ☐ for educational purposes including research papers ☐ , publications ☐, exhibitions ☐, World Wide Web ☐, and presentations ☐. (Check all that apply)

By giving my permission, I do not give up any copyright or performance rights that I may hold.

My participation is voluntary and I may refuse at any time to participate further. One copy of the tapes/transcripts of my interview(s) will be given to me. Except as provided above, all other copies will be_____ after the course is completed.

Further restrictions (if any) on the use of the materials:
_____
_____
_____
_____
_____

I am of legal age to provide consent.

_____
Signature of Participant and date

_____
Signature of Interviewer and date

Figure 1.1   Interview release form

6. ***Think critically about oral sources.*** Information obtained through interviews is often reliable, but like all historical evidence it should be subject to critical evaluation. Be aware that your subjects may not remember events exactly as they happened, and that their opinions may well not agree. If possible, compare their stories with the stories that other people tell you, as well as any written sources that may be available. Written sources are not necessarily more reliable than oral sources, but writing can often be a more effective way to preserve a version of history.

7. ***Cultivate your skills both as an interviewer and as an interpreter of interviews.*** It takes a lot of practice to learn how to work with interview subjects. The best interviewers are usually the most experienced, but even they were beginners once. For a thorough guide to the process, see Valerie Raleigh Yow, *Recording Oral History: A Guide for the Humanities and Social Sciences*, 3rd ed. (Toronto: Altamira Press, 2014). For a shorter guide that focuses more specifically on the practical details of oral history see Edward D. Ives, *The Tape-Recorded Interview: A Manual for Fieldworkers in Folklore and Oral History*, 2nd ed. (Knoxville: University of Tennessee Press, 1995).

Once your interviewing is complete, use the evidence you have gathered just as you would use any historical source—as long as the use is in accordance with whatever guidelines have been set in your consent form. Exercise your academic integrity: it is not your role to sugar-coat or otherwise distort your materials or your findings, but do be respectful of your subjects' meanings and intentions.

Reading Response Journal

A reading journal assignment is designed to allow you to develop your own thoughts about course materials without the constraints that come with an essay assignment, although some instructors assign reading journals as bases for later papers. Unless otherwise instructed, you can use informal language and your own approach and arrangement, and you can let your thoughts run free. Keep some guidelines in mind, however. If your instructor is to read some or all of your material, keep your language clean, your thoughts focused, and your points clear. This assignment is about thinking, not random musing.

Briefly summarize the reading, making sure to identify the most important points, any contentious points, and any points you do not understand. If you are responding to more than one piece, think about any similarities and differences of focus and opinion and consider the reasons. Are the arguments or approaches valid?

If appropriate to the assignment, you might (within limits) consider your own reactions: for example, do you find the material interesting, dull, surprising, amusing, upsetting, intriguing? Why do you feel this way? Emotional responses can be interesting, and you may certainly include them (unless your instructor rules them out). However, responses based on historical knowledge, on other reading, or on experience are more relevant, and these are what your instructor will be looking for.

One final note: try to set aside a regular time for your journal. It may be tempting to let the journal slide when you have more immediate deadlines, but you will regret putting the journal work off when you have to catch up on it several weeks or months later. You will not be able to do a good and thoughtful job under those circumstances. Besides, the whole point of a response journal is to record your thinking as it develops over time and help you to consolidate your understanding of the materials as the course progresses. Writing several weeks' worth of journal entries all at once defeats the purpose and deprives you of the benefits. Another advantage of diligent journal work will become obvious when you have to prepare for papers and exams. A carefully completed journal, with good summaries of course readings, will save you a great deal of effort later on.

Essay Exam

Most history exams include an essay component, and a little planning can help you a lot. Listen carefully in class for any clues your instructor gives in the few weeks before exam time: many drop hints for those who are paying attention. Try not to leave your studying until the last moment. Set aside a regular time to study and review, then keep to your schedule. This will be far more useful than any last-minute cramming. Watch for recurring themes, ideas, people, or events frequently emphasized by the book or instructor.

An especially useful study method is to compose your own essay questions and then write model answers to them. For example, if a major course theme has been the development of federal–provincial relations in the nineteenth century, you could compose a question about the shifting power dynamics between the two levels of government. Then you could decide on and study the major "sign-post" events and factors to discuss, such as the rise of the provincial rights movement, the New Brunswick schools questions of the 1870s, the Ontario boundary dispute of the 1880s, the Northwest Rebellion, the formation of the Parti national, the Manitoba schools question, and the Laurier–Greenway compromise. Your question will probably not be identical to anything on the exam paper, but you will almost certainly have studied in detail the material necessary to answer your instructor's questions.

When writing the exam, read each question carefully and think about what a thorough but focused answer needs to cover. Take a few moments to write a brief outline. Remember that every essay requires an introduction and conclusion, a **thesis** statement, logical ordering of points, and sufficient evidence to support your arguments. Focus on the question in front of you: don't try to change it into a question you can answer more easily, and don't pad your answer with a lot of unnecessary information just because you know it. You need to show your instructor that you understand the material so well that you are able not just to regurgitate but to develop your own thoughts based on all the evidence. Be aware of any constraints of time or length and try to leave a few minutes to proofread, to make sure that both your ideas and your handwriting are clear.

Practical Strategies

No matter what type of exam you are taking, it will go better if you have a strategy. Obviously, you are more likely to do well if you have worked hard all term and studied diligently for the exam. Apart from any other benefit, this will give you the confidence you need to get a good sleep the night before the exam and arrive well rested. "All-nighters" rarely produce good exam results.

Also make sure you know what you are allowed to bring to the exam. Scrap paper? Something to drink? Should you take a sweater? Tissues? Will you be allowed a bathroom break? Prepare beforehand so that you won't be distracted during the exam.

When you get the exam, don't just jump in and start writing. Take a few moments to read it carefully. Pay attention to any directions regarding the length or format of your answers. As you read, think about how much time you have and assign a ballpark time limit to each part of the exam so that you will not feel overly rushed. First, identify the easiest questions and if you can answer them very quickly, do that now. If there are some that will be easy but will need a little time to compose, set them aside for now.

Next, look at the rest of the questions. If you think some will be really difficult, set them aside as well and just let them percolate in the back of your brain for a while. You may find that, as you relax into the exam, you will start remembering things that you thought you had forgotten. In the meantime, complete first the questions that are neither the easiest nor the hardest. Then go back to the easy ones, but resist any temptation to spend too much time or space on the answers just because you know them so well. Finally, turn to the hardest questions. Following this approach allows you to use your time effectively and ensure that you don't leave any "easy" marks on the table.

Above all, have confidence and remember that an exam is a chance to show how much you know. Your professor will be looking for the correct answers to straight factual questions, of course, but also for evidence that you have thought about the material and made it your own. If you really have worked properly all semester, you might even find that you enjoy writing the exam.

> **TIP!** If you've worked hard all semester and studied carefully, relax—you know this stuff!

Research Proposal

A research proposal, submitted before you begin writing a more extensive essay, can be a very useful exercise. It gives you the opportunity to start work in good time, to think carefully about your topic, and to get feedback from your instructor, all of which will help you produce a strong final paper. Just keep in mind that such assignments are not as easy as they may look. Thoughtful and careful work now will make the writing process easier and will give your instructor a better opportunity to guide you. Allow yourself plenty of time. You will need to think about a subject, search out relevant sources, and read them in enough detail to know how they relate to your topic and to each other.

Generally, a research proposal will include a title, a short description of your research topic and its significance, a list (in proper bibliographical format) of the sources you intend to use and how you intend to use them, and a provisional thesis statement. The final paper may not conform exactly to your proposal, since your instructor's feedback and your own further research may lead you to new sources and ideas. The paper should not differ from the proposal too much, however, or the project will become meaningless.

Annotated Bibliography

This assignment may be either a stand-alone project or a first step towards an eventual paper. In the latter case, it is very like a research proposal except that it concentrates more on assessing the works in question than on discussing the paper's thesis or direction. You will still need to keep your thesis in mind, however, to make the most of the project and to ensure that your **bibliography** is coherent and focused, not just a random list of works.

For the assignment itself, you will likely be asked to propose a title or a topic for research. Be sure to present each book, article, or document title in proper bibliographical format. In

> **TIP!** See Appendix B for details on formatting bibliographical entries.

each case, summarize the main points of the work and evaluate its major strengths and weaknesses. If required, explain briefly how you intend to use each work in your research paper. See pages 42–43 for an example of an annotated bibliography.

Historical Research Paper

Traditionally, the most common assignment in history courses has been the research paper, and much of the remainder of this book will focus on this type of assignment so as to illustrate the research and writing process. In this assignment, the student explores in some detail a specific topic related to the course in order to say something of significance about the topic. This might sound quite intimidating, especially if the instructor does not give you a specific topic, but it is also exciting: this assignment allows you to explore a significant topic and to draw your own conclusions based on the evidence you uncover. But how to start? Let's assume that your choice is free and the only restriction is that the topic relates clearly to the contents of the course.

First: Explore Your Interests

When someone at a party asks you what you're interested in, you probably don't stop and reflect: you answer with a quick one-liner. When your history instructor asks you to choose an essay topic, you can take advantage of the opportunity to think about your interests in more depth.

As a student, you may be drawn to the history of medicine because you want to become a doctor; or the history of physics may interest you because you are concerned about nuclear proliferation. Perhaps some historians have sparked your interest through their teaching or writing. When you have the chance to choose your topic, you can use it to explore questions that are significant to you. The research paper is the perfect vehicle for this. Chapter 2 will look at how to use your personal interest to generate a focused research topic.

REVIEW

1. Most history assignments use similar techniques and approaches.
2. Allow plenty of time for history assignments.
3. Prepare carefully for exams: don't try to cram.
4. If you can choose your own research topic, choose something you find interesting.

Starting Your Assignment

Move from a Historical Interest to a Research Topic

How do you convert your historical interest into a research topic? First, remembering that your topic must clearly be relevant to the course, look for a small story within your broad range of interests. Think about what it is, specifically, that you enjoy learning about. Let's say that as a child you were fascinated by stories of explorers such as Alexander Mackenzie and Simon Fraser; as a teenager you read everything you could find on the fur trade; and last year your favourite course was an introduction to the Metis people of the Canadian West that touched on the dramatic story of Louis Riel and the Northwest Resistance. Maybe you could write an essay on the history of the Metis?

Unfortunately, this is the sort of broad topic that is better suited to a textbook than to a short essay. Chances are that your time is limited and your teacher has set a page limit for your essay in any case. How can you find a topic that will let you explore your interests but will also accommodate your limitations? Many resources available online or in the library can help you to narrow down your topic.

> **TIP!** Most history assignments will require you to go through similar research processes.

Using Electronic Resources

Although history professors usually prefer published sources, the reality is that most students today will begin their research online. There are many worthy online resources, from books and articles to library

catalogues and pictures of art and architecture. (See Appendix C, "Suggested History Resources," for some examples.) There are also many unworthy sites. The trick is to distinguish between them.

It takes a great deal of time and effort to produce, print, and distribute a book, or even a journal article. Typically, a work of history that is to be published must first be approved not only by a team of editors but by several **peer reviewers**, that is, highly trained specialists in the field. Web publishing, on the other hand, is cheap, easy, and often free of quality controls. This is why many instructors mistrust online sources and some insist that their students include some traditional books and journal articles, preferably written by recognized specialists in the field. So how do you use online resources wisely?

One way to find a useful website is to use a high-quality search engine such as Google or the more specialized Google Scholar (scholar.google.com), which gives you access to scholarly and governmental documents and publications. Start with a keyword search. In a keyword search, it's important to use distinctive words. Type in "Metis" and you will get millions of entries. The results will be more narrowly focused if you include more terms: for instance, "Metis history" or even "Metis history Riel." The most useful hits are likely to come near the top of the list, but be sure to look carefully through at least the first few pages. In the course of scanning these entries you may think of additional terms that will allow you to refine your search even further. Search engines don't understand your thought process, so the more specific your search terms are, the more relevant the results will be.

Check the address and sponsor. When you find a promising site, note the address, the author, the title, the owner of the domain, and the date of publication. This will not only help you to evaluate the site, but will allow you to give a proper **citation** later, when you are writing. Beware of sites that are trying to sell you a product or service, or that leave you wondering "who wrote this?" Often the best sites are affiliated with academic, government, or non-profit institutions. At the very least, the content of these sites has been judged acceptable by the sponsoring organizations, and in many cases it will represent the official view. On the subject of Louis Riel, for example, *The Dictionary* *of Canadian Biography*, published by the University of Toronto Press and Les Presses de l'Université Laval, has an informative biographical web page on Riel's life and legacy at www.biographi.ca/en/bio/riel_louis_1844_85_11E.html.

By contrast, you should be particularly cautious with web addresses ending in ".com" or ".co": these are commercial sites, and anybody with a credit card can create one. This is not to say that all commercial sites are bad (or that all academic sites are good), but checking the extension is one way to begin sorting through a long list of possible sites.

Has the material on the site been published in print? Many sites begin as print sources, or are published in both print and electronic editions. The quality of these sites is often high, because print media tend to have relatively strict quality controls.

Is the information on the site available elsewhere? There are now some outstanding websites associated with universities, museums, and historical archives. In these cases, the actual sources of the information published online are available in physical form. Thus selected but extensive excerpts from the transcript of the trial of Louis Riel are available online at http://law2.umkc.edu/faculty/projects/ftrials/riel/riel.html and the complete transcript, along with a detailed introductory essay, can also be found in Desmond Morton's *The Queen v. Louis Riel*, published by the University of Toronto Press in 1974.

Be skeptical. Some websites are invaluable for historians, some are completely useless, and many are just mediocre. How can you tell the difference? Assess the tone of the writing. Is it scholarly? Or is the author ranting, trying to convert you to some belief or opinion? Does the coverage seem thorough and balanced? Is there a clear point of view? If so, is there significant evidence to substantiate the point of view? Is it consistent with evidence from other sources? Is the evidence used fairly and reasonably? Can it be verified? Are there any obvious factual errors? Is the site presented by scholars whose names and affiliations you recognize and respect? Pay attention as well to the site's organization and writing. Is the organization clear and logical? Can you spot any errors in grammar or punctuation?

When in doubt, ask your professor. None of the criteria listed above is enough on their own to determine a site's reliability, but together they can help. If you still have doubts about a particular site, ask your professor to check it for you, perhaps via e-mail message containing the Internet address of the website in question. It's always better to ask about a source in advance than to be criticized for it after you have turned in the paper.

What about Wikipedia? Wikipedia is a collaborative encyclopedia made up of entries that can be written or edited by anyone with access to a computer. In other words, the material it contains can come from anywhere and can be modified or changed—added to or subtracted from—and that is where the danger lies. Much of the material on Wikipedia is properly referenced, and much is reliable. Some, however, is not: there have been several supposedly reliable historical entries that even turned out to be completely fictional. Because there are few quality controls, the reliability is not consistent and academic opinions on its usefulness differ. You can certainly ask your professor if Wikipedia is an acceptable starting point for a research project. If it is, looking at the site may give you an initial idea of the scope of your topic, some ideas about areas for research, and perhaps some sources to investigate. But Wikipedia alone cannot serve as the basis for a real research paper, and in any case you will need to verify any material you find there by checking other sources. Since most historians begin their research with published sources, so should you. Now is the time to go to the library.

> **TIP!** Don't believe everything you read— check your facts in multiple sources.

Using Print Sources

Visit the reading room of any good library and you will find a collection of reference works—encyclopedias, dictionaries, and textbooks—covering a broad range of interests and topics. (Many encyclopedias and dictionaries are also available online.)

Encyclopedias. A good encyclopedia can give you a broad overview of a topic. It will contain basic explanations as well as hints about related subjects. Just keep in mind that most encyclopedia articles can't provide anything more than an introduction. They are not substantial enough to serve as the basis of a paper. Nevertheless, *The Canadian Encyclopedia* does contain a useful summary of Metis history, including a series of links to other sites and a **bibliography**. In this case, an encyclopedia article could help to jump-start a research project.

Dictionaries. Dictionaries also offer a quick way to explore some topics. There are three different types of dictionary, each of which has its own special uses. *Prescriptive* dictionaries like *Webster's* will tell you how words should be used; *descriptive* dictionaries like *The Canadian Oxford Dictionary* will tell you how words are actually used; and *historical* dictionaries like *The Oxford English Dictionary* will tell you how words have been used over time. Some, such as *The Gage Canadian Dictionary*, include both prescriptive and descriptive features.

In the case of the Metis, dictionaries probably have little to offer, but they are still worth a look. The meaning of "Metis" is clear enough, and so are its origins in Canadian usage. You may be interested to find that *The Oxford English Dictionary* identifies a variety of nineteenth-century occasions when the word "Metis" was used to denote mixed race people of White and First Nations descent but this information doesn't appear to raise any interesting research questions.

> **TIP!** Depending on your topic, texts from other disciplines such as sociology or geography may also be useful.

Textbooks. Some textbooks may contain useful surveys of your topic, and they are sure to contain bibliographies. For information on the Metis, more than one type of text could prove to be useful. A textbook on world history might include interesting material on indigenous peoples, while a textbook on Canadian history would provide more detail on the specific Canadian context. Be sure to check textbook bibliographies for further references.

The Academic Library

Perhaps the best place to start a research assignment is the library in your own institution, where you will find a wealth of materials. Since an academic library is designed for student and faculty research, the resources that are available to you will almost certainly be more extensive than those easily available in even an excellent public library. Suppose you wanted to conduct a search for "Louis Riel" in your library. You are likely to find many hits including both general and specialized reference works online and perhaps in hard copy, books on the shelves (usually called "the stacks"), e-books, journal articles, movies, and so on. Your first stop should be the reference works. Note that some academic libraries no longer keep separate reference rooms full of such works because most major reference sources such as encyclopedias are easily available online. You may also find hard copies of reference works stored in the stacks. Beyond encyclopedias and general dictionaries, you might look at more specialized sources such as *The Dictionary of Canadian Biography*, for example, which will give you the main outline of Riel's life and his significance. Another useful source might be *The Oxford Companion to Canadian History*, which includes articles on Riel himself as well as on some of the events in which he was involved. Sources such as these will help you to identify specific directions for research, such as Riel's role in the founding of Manitoba, his involvement in the Northwest Resistance (also known as the Northwest Rebellion), Metis relations with the First Nations, the legality of his trial, and so on. These sources may also list some of the most important historical works on his life.

Ask a Librarian

By the time you have exhausted your library's main reference collection, whether online or in the library itself, you will have a sense of Riel's "story" and perhaps an idea of what aspect you would like to explore in a paper. You may also have accumulated a list of possible authors and titles. Now you will need to start looking in the library catalogue for the titles of books and articles that are available to you. Library catalogues can be a tremendous help in the search for works on a particular subject. Most are now computerized and accessible online. However, since library holdings change constantly, it's a good idea to talk with a librarian—a research specialist—before you begin to search the catalogue. Librarians are the unsung heroes of the historical world and historians depend heavily on them, because they not only preserve information but also know how it is organized and how to access it. They can be an enormous help to historians and students in finding what they need. This is particularly important to emphasize in today's world, when electronic access to information is increasing exponentially, ways to access it are changing constantly, and academic libraries are arranging their materials in a variety of ways—as one reference librarian phrases the situation, "It's the wild west out there."[8] Reference librarians are experts in electronic searches, and most will be happy to show you how to begin. You will save yourself a lot of time and maximize the likelihood of finding good sources by consulting a librarian at the outset of your project.

Explore the Library Catalogue

The key to searching a computerized catalogue is understanding how the information is organized. As mentioned above, not all libraries arrange their materials or their lists the same way, but there are still some general rules to rely on. Most items in the library are listed by author, title, and subject heading. In order to find the right headings, start with a keyword search. Again, the choice of words is crucial. "Metis history Riel" will probably take you to many works, each of which will have subject headings. Click on the subject headings to link to other works on the same subject. Please note that subject searches are different from keyword searches. A keyword search may turn up your terms in many different orders, but subject headings are fixed by the US Library of Congress. You won't hit a subject heading unless you type in its exact wording. (All librarians will be able to explain to you how to search for Library of Congress subject headings.) Once you come across a useful subject heading, follow the links to other headings. Click on author and title links to identify related works.

Explore Online Library Resources

One advantage of doing an electronic search at an academic library is that the resources it makes available are likely to be worthwhile. Talk with your reference librarians about the **databases** available through your institution. You may be able to browse through them or even to access their holdings directly through your library's online catalogue. If so, think about broad topic areas to check for your particular project: there may be databases not only for history, but also for anthropology, business, politics, and Canadian, Aboriginal, or women's studies.

While small college libraries cannot afford all the resources that their counterparts at big research universities can, several types of services are commonly available. Along with encyclopedias and dictionaries, issues of historical journals are generally available online and indexes of articles and unpublished dissertations are available by library subscription. In addition, many books that are not kept in your own library can be viewed or even borrowed in e-versions through centralized websites of library books such as the Canadian Electronic Library and WorldCat, which gives you access to thousands of library catalogues all over the world. See Figure 2.1 for WorldCat's initial results from a simple "Louis Riel" search.

Notice that WorldCat allows you to filter results by choosing what types of materials you want to look at. Do you want books and articles, or only articles? Do you want only items that can be downloaded? Would you be interested in videos? Make all these choices and more by checking the boxes on the left of the screen. You can also get more specific results by refining your search. For instance, if you enter "Louis Riel trial" you will get references that relate specifically to that aspect of Riel's story (see Figure 2.2).

Now that WorldCat has given you a start, you can follow its links to view or download books, articles, documents, movies, or whatever you have chosen. You can filter your results further if you like, for instance by searching for "Louis Riel trial lawyers" and just keep

Search WorldCat

louis Riel 🔍

Search

Advanced Search Find a Library

Search results for 'louis Riel'

Format

☑ All Formats (2,579)
☐ Book (1366)
 – ☐ Microform (328)
 – ☐ eBook (284)
 – ☐ Thesis/dissertation (62)
☐ Article (506)
 – ☐ Chapter (60)
 – ☐ Downloadable article (18)
☐ Video (205)
 – ☐ VHS (111)
 – ☐ DVD (66)
 – ☐ eVideo (16)
 – ☐ Film (2)
☐ Archival material (159)
 – ☐ Downloadable archival material (130)
☐ Music (134)
 – ☐ CD (75)
 – ☐ LP (30)
 – ☐ Cassette (19)
 – ☐ eMusic (3)
Show more ...

Refine Your Search

Author
Louis Riel (115)
Canadian Broadcas... (43)
Canada (33)
Mark Starowicz (25)
Joseph-Adolphe Ch... (21)
Show more ...

Year
2009 (95)
2001 (102)
1985 (115)
1886 (182)
1885 (99)
Show more ...

Language
English (1569)
French (625)
Undetermined (165)
German (10)
Multiple languages (8)
Show more ...

Content
Biography (243)
Fiction (58)
Non-Fiction (2521)

Audience

Results **1-10** of about **2,579** (.26 seconds)   « First ‹ Prev 1 2 3 Next ›

Select All Clear All   Save to: [New List] ⌄   Save   Sort by: Relevance ⌄   Save Search

☐ 1. 480838
       1
       Louis Riel.
       by George Francis Gillman Stanley
       📕 Book View all formats and languages »
       Language: English
       Publisher: Toronto, Ryerson Press [©1963]
       Database: WorldCat

       View all editions »

☐ 2. 3843872
       2
       Louis Riel
       by Rosemary Neering
       📕 Book : Biography View all formats and languages »
       Language: English
       Publisher: Don Mills, Ont. : Fitzhenry & Whiteside, ©1977.
       Database: WorldCat

       View all editions »

☐ 3. 37001604
       3
       Louis Riel
       by Thomas Flanagan
       📕 Book : Biography View all formats and languages »
       Language: English
       Publisher: Ottawa : Canadian Historical Association, 1992.
       Database: WorldCat

       View all editions »

☐ 4. 14965715
       4
       Louis Riel
       by Harry Somers; Mavor Moore; Jacques Languirand; Victor Feldbrill; Canadian Opera Company. Chorus.; National Arts Centre. Orchestra.
       🎵 Music LP View all formats and languages »
       Language: English

       Publisher: Toronto, Ont., Canada : Centrediscs, 1985.
       Database: WorldCat

       View all editions »

☐ 5. 70676004
       5
       Louis Riel
       by Terry Barber
       📕 Book : Biography : Juvenile audience View all formats and languages »
       Language: English
       Publisher: [Edmonton, Alta.?] : Grass Roots Press, ©2006.
       Database: WorldCat

       View all editions »

Figure 2.1   WorldCat search results for "Louis Riel"

Source: Courtesy OCLC Online Computer Library Center, Inc.

Search WorldCat

| Louis Riel trial | 🔍 |

Search

Advanced Search Find a Library

Search results for **'Louis Riel trial'**

ℹ Format

✓ All Formats (272)
☐ Article (121)
   ☐ Chapter (26)
   ☐ Downloadable article (2)
☐ Book (112)
   ☐ eBook (35)
   ☐ Microform (30)
   ☐ Thesis/dissertation (3)
☐ Video (28)
   ☐ VHS (14)
   ☐ DVD (9)
   ☐ eVideo (3)
☐ Downloadable archival material (4)
☐ Cassette (3)
☐ Computer file (3)
☐ Image (2)
Show more ...

ℹ Refine Your Search

Author

Louis Riel (13)
Canadian Broadcas... (10)
Canada (7)
Edward Blake (6)
Alexander Campbell (4)
Show more ...

Year

2007 (16)
2002 (15)
2001 (14)
1886 (31)
1885 (15)
Show more ...

Language

English (226)
French (19)
Undetermined (10)
German (1)

Content

Biography (14)
Fiction (2)
Non-Fiction (270)

Audience

Juvenile (5)
Non-Juvenile (267)

Topic

History & Auxilia... (58)
Law (23)

Results **1-10** of about **272** (**.68** seconds)   « First ‹ Prev 1 2 3 Next ›

Select All Clear All   **Save to:** [New List] ⇕ [Save] Sort by: Relevance ⇕ [Save Search]

☐ 1.
   26717396
   1
   The Queen v Louis Riel.
   by Louis Riel
   📖 Book View all formats and languages »
   Language: English
   Publisher: New York : Gryphon Editions, 1992.
   Database: WorldCat

   View all editions »

☐ 2.
   576766390
   2
   The Queen vs. Louis Riel, accused and convicted of the crime of high treason ; report of trial at Regina.--Appeal to the Court of Queen's Bench, Manitoba.--Appeal to the Privy Council, England.--Petition for medical examination of the convict.--List of petitions for commutation of sentence, Ottawa.
   by Louis Riel; Manitoba. Court of Queen's Bench.
   📄 eBook : Document View all formats and languages »
   Language: English
   Publisher: Ottawa : Printed by the Queen's printer, 1886.
   Database: WorldCat

   View all editions »

☐ 3.
   443032
   3
   The trial of Louis Riel;
   by John Coulter
   📖 Book View all formats and languages »
   Language: English
   Publisher: [Ottawa] Oberon Press, 1968.
   Database: WorldCat

   View all editions »

☐ 4.
   1179500
   4
   The trial of Louis Riel [a play]
   by Frederick G Walsh
   📖 Book View all formats and languages »
   Language: English
   Publisher: Fargo, North Dakota Institute for Regional Studies, 1965.
   Database: WorldCat

   View all editions »

☐ 5.
   506065954
   5
   [Trial of Louis Riel]

Figure 2.2   Refined search results in WorldCat

going until you reach the destination you want. If an item you want is not available online, perhaps you can access it through Interlibrary Loan—ask your librarian about this service.

Another useful site, available by personal or institutional subscription, is Oxford Bibliographies Online (www.oxfordbibliographiesonline.com). Search this site within categories such as African Studies, Medieval Studies, Military History or Islamic Studies. There is no separate category for Canadian history, but depending on your topic you can find many references to Canadian history under the more generic categories such as Atlantic History.

Colleges and universities buy access to controlled websites, library portals, and databases so that you can use them for research. Databases typically give you access to online periodicals that you will not find through a Google-type search; you can usually search for particular journals, subjects, authors, topics, and keywords. Once you find useful resources, you can print them or e-mail them to yourself. But you should be aware that computerized indexes may not list articles that were written before the 1980s, and that the indexes themselves may be out of date by a year or two. If they are available to you, it pays to check the "hard copy" indexes and tables of contents for titles that are either very old or very new.

A variety of online services will search through multiple databases that used to exist only in print form, such as Books In Print, the Humanities Index, the Social Science Index, and Dissertation Abstracts (a guide to over a million doctoral dissertations from all over the world), although some of these databases allow full access only through libraries that subscribe to the service.

College libraries subscribe to many different online services such as EBSCOhost, which gives you access to articles from a huge variety of journals. Similarly, JSTOR, "The Scholarly Journal Archive," offers access to back issues of scholarly (mostly American and British) journals in many fields, including history (some of JSTOR's holdings go back as far as the seventeenth century). Libraries purchase subscriptions to specific groups of publications in JSTOR. The same is true of ProQuest, a database that allows you to search for dissertations as well as articles and will eventually provide access to several billion images. The University of Illinois' History Cooperative site provides easy access to full-text journal articles, historical map collections, and historians' web links. Historical Abstracts allows you to find abstracts (summaries of the most important points) of articles and book reviews from more than 2000 journals from all over the world; for Canadian as well as US history, look under "American History and Life, File 38." Project Muse (available only through subscribing libraries) carries an online database, searchable by keyword or phrase, of more than 400 journals, including the *Canadian Historical Review* and the *Journal of Canadian Studies*.

Some online search services deliver the full texts of articles. If the full text is not immediately available, the article may be requested through Interlibrary Loan. Most Interlibrary Loan services now deliver articles electronically.

> **TIP!** If you download published articles, choose to do it in such a way that the original page numbers appear on your screen—your reference librarian can show you how to do this. It will be important if you quote from or refer to the article in your own assignment.

Sources for Canadian History

A wide variety of reference works and bibliographies on Canadian topics are available in most college and university libraries, and most can be accessed in e-versions. Bibliographies list books and articles that focus on particular topics. They may be arranged alphabetically, geographically, or chronologically by subject matter or date of publication, and these categories are often cross-referenced. You can use them to get ideas of titles to search for in your own library, through Interlibrary Loan or, more likely, online. General bibliographies include *Canadian History: A Reader's Guide*, *The Oxford Companion to Canadian History and Literature* (and its *Supplement*), *Introducing Canada: An Annotated Bibliography of Canadian History in English* (not available online), and *Canadian Reference Sources: An Annotated*

Bibliography.[9] In addition to simple lists of bibliographical sources in various topic areas, many of these works contain articles on places, individuals, groups, political parties, governmental policies, business affairs, and so on.

You might also check to see whether your library has any more general historical bibliographies, such as the Historical Association's *Annual Bulletin of Historical Literature,* which publishes reviews of recent books, journals, and journal articles as well as special sections on specific areas (such as "the Americas") and specific time periods.[10] In addition, university libraries sometimes have bibliographical collections specific to particular regions, which may be worth checking. Depending on your area of research, it may also be useful to check the holdings of municipal and provincial archives, public libraries, and museums.

Once you have a more specific idea of the area you want to research, you might also check for specialized bibliographies. If you were interested in women's history, for example, you could look at *Changing Women, Changing History: A Bibliography of the History of Women in Canada.* For First Nations' history you would want to check references such as *The Ethnographic Bibliography of North America.* For military history, you might consult *The Canadian Military Experience 1867–1995: A Bibliography.* Perhaps you are interested in regional history? In that case you might look for books such as *A Bibliography of British Columbia* or (for even more local content) *The Vancouver Centennial Bibliography.*[11] Similar works exist for many other regions, for instance the Atlantic Canada Portal that can be found at atlanticportal.hil.unb. ca/biblio This portal is also associated with an online bibliography of over 20,000 titles maintained by *Acadiensis: The Journal of the History of the Atlantic Region.* In addition, you can easily find the Atlantic Canada Virtual Archives.

Among the general Canadian reference works at your disposal are *The Canadian Encyclopedia* and *The Dictionary of Canadian Biography* (both available online as well as in print), *The Oxford Companion to Canadian History, The Encyclopedia of Canada's Peoples, Canadian Who's Who, The Canadian Annual Review of Politics and Public Affairs,* and *The Fitzhenry and Whiteside Book of Canadian Facts and Dates.*[12] In many cases the articles in these books contain lists of sources, so be sure to check them for additional ideas. Another important reference work is *The Historical Atlas of Canada*, which has been

> **TIP!** A great way to search online for relevant titles is to enter your topic into the search box and add the word "bibliographies."

published in a three-volume set as well as a concise edition, and which includes short articles and bibliographies for most of its maps.[13] Regional or local encyclopedias and atlases can be useful as well, depending on your topic.

Periodicals and scholarly journals can also be valuable sources for Canadian history. Probably the best way to find relevant articles is to search the various periodical indexes. These list articles from journals, magazines, and newspapers, and they are arranged alphabetically both by subject and by author. College libraries can give you access to *The Canadian Periodical Index*, *The Canadian Magazine Index*, *The Social Sciences Index*, *The Humanities Index*, and *The Canadian Index*, all of which are reasonably easy to use. *The Canadian Index*, for example, lists citations for articles from several hundred journals, both scholarly and popular, covering a broad range of topic areas. It is particularly useful for biographical information not just on figures such as politicians and military leaders, but on people such as artists and authors, both historical and contemporary. Most indexes allow you to search for keywords as well as specific names or subject areas.

If you find articles in journals that your institution does not carry, you can usually access them online or through Interlibrary Loan. Some historical journals, such as the *Canadian Historical Review*, have their own indexes for ease of research. Be sure to find out whether any specialized journals might offer material relevant to your topic. Journals such as *Urban History Review*, *Prairie Forum*, *Newfoundland Studies*, *Acadiensis* (devoted to the Atlantic region), the *Canadian Journal of Native Studies*, and *Labour/Le Travail* fall into this category.

Finally, a few words about electronic searches and sources. In addition to the online sources outlined above, there are many other sites that deal directly with Canadian historical material. The Library and Archives Canada site, for instance, offers what it calls "the Canadian national catalogue" of the published materials held in more than 1,300 libraries across the country. This is an excellent site for locating specific material. It also offers links to resources such as other federal government sites, the Portrait Gallery of Canada, the online *Dictionary of Canadian Biography*, the Canadian Genealogy Centre, and an excellent research tool called ArchiviaNet that can take you to a number of searchable data and photograph collections. You can find Library and Archives at www.collectionscanada.ca. Another useful resource is Canada in the Making, at www.canadiana.org/citm/. Based on the Government Documents section of the Early Canadiana Online collection, it offers narrative texts and links to primary sources, as well as collections of related materials to help you explore themes such as "Aboriginal Treaties" or "Pioneers and Immigrants." Canadiana. org, an organization of members such as libraries, provincial governments, and universities, offers easy access to early Canadian printed materials at eco.canadiana.ca. The Our Roots project (www.ourroots. ca), concentrates on Canadian local history materials. Finally, most general textbooks on Canadian history contain lists of publicly available sites that are worth checking.

Approach Your Topic from a Particular Angle

A library at a large university may contain hundreds of items on the subject of the Metis, and it could also have special collections of manuscripts and artifacts. Even a small library may have several dozen items, and it will certainly provide digital access to many more. Don't be discouraged. You simply need to bring more focus to your topic.

Think back to the books you have read and the courses you have taken. If you like reading biographies, then you might want to focus on an individual who made a significant contribution to the field. If you prefer social history, you might choose a topic along the lines of class, gender, or race. You might be especially interested in the history of a particular place or time period, or perhaps a process, such as the formation of an institution. Keep working on your searches until you have identified a reasonably focused topic and a manageable number of resources that you can use as the basis of your research.

Suppose you are still considering writing about Louis Riel. While searching the library catalogue for books, you decide to look for a biography, and find J.M. Bumsted's *Louis Riel v. Canada*, published in 2001. You also do a search for articles in peer-reviewed scholarly journals and realize quickly that there are a host of them. Skimming their titles, you notice that several themes crop up repeatedly, such as Riel's role in the Northwest Rebellion of 1885, his mental status and his trial and execution. Clearly, these are areas that historians continue to find significant.

> **TIP!** Think carefully about how much you can handle within the page limits of your assignment, and narrow your focus accordingly.

Go to the Library and Do Some Background Reading

Searching cannot be done exclusively from a computer terminal or a card catalogue. It's time to go to the library stacks. Locate Bumsted's book and look around. On the same shelf you will almost certainly find several other books relating to Riel. Pull them out and take a look: skim the indexes, read the prologues and conclusions, and keep an eye open for specific topic areas that seem interesting to explore. Check the bibliographies of all the books you find, even those that are not very useful in themselves, for promising titles.

As you define your topic, you will find yourself moving back and forth between the catalogue and the stacks. Go back to the catalogue and search under "Riel" and "rebellion." Here, among many items, you notice several promising titles: for example, Dan Asfar and Tim Chodan's *Louis Riel* (Edmonton: Folklore Publishers, 2003) tells the story of Riel's life and death and outlines his two conflicts with the Canadian government. George R.D. Goulet's *The Trial of Louis Riel: Justice and Mercy Denied* (Calgary: Tellwell Publishing, 1999) is a detailed study of the trial, written by a retired lawyer. Because it lacks **footnotes**, an index, and a detailed list of sources, Asfar and Chodan's book falls into the category of popular rather than scholarly history and therefore is not suitable as a source for an academic paper. (It is also written from a very definite point of view rather than from a position of objectivity.) Goulet's book includes reference notes, a detailed index and a substantial bibliography from which you can draw titles to search. While Goulet is not a trained historian, as a very experienced former lawyer he could certainly be seen as an expert on legal matters. Note also, however, that according to the information on the back cover, he is descended from one of Riel's close associates—when reading Goulet you will need to keep your eyes open for biases.

Your search for scholarly articles also leads to some promising titles, such as Paul Groarke's "The Trial and Execution of Louis Riel: Defending My Country Northwest," published in the *Canadian Journal of Native Studies* in July 2013. Now you have sources that can point you in further directions.

Browse for More Sources

There is only one way to make an informed choice about a topic: browse through the potential source materials, whether in the library stacks or online. Look for both quantity and quality. Are there enough sources to write this paper, or are there so many that you will have to define your topic more narrowly? It's also important to consider when various sources were published. Are you finding the most recent work in the field? A book that was published decades ago could well be out of date. Use your judgment, however: if all of the recent authors refer to the same older work, it's probably worth your while also to take a look at it. When thinking about Riel, George F.G. Stanley's *Louis Riel*, originally published in 1963, falls into this category.

It's usually a good idea to start with a narrow base of sources and build it into a broader base. Therefore, try to find some of the sources in Asfar and Chodan's very short bibliography, and as you dig more deeply, draw on the longer lists provided by Goulet. As you search, you will find more clues that will lead you to further sources. Just keep in mind that there are limits both to your time and to the length of your paper. You don't need to locate every potential source right now: just enough to get you started.

Distinguishing Primary Sources from Secondary Works

Not all sources are created equal. In particular, historians distinguish between primary and secondary sources.

Primary sources. A primary source is one that originates in the time period under study. Such sources take many forms, and not all of them are documents: as well as personal memoirs and correspondence, government or church documents, and transcripts of legal proceedings, they may include oral histories and traditions, archaeological and biological evidence, and visual materials such as sculptures, paintings, and photographs. Primary sources, particularly documents, are the foundations of nearly all historians' work, and your professor may instruct you to use them as well.

Each kind of primary source must be considered on its own terms. Historians used to think that materials such as government documents were inherently more reliable than others. But even government documents are not entirely straightforward or objective. Like all sources, they reveal some things and obscure others. This means that you need to think carefully not just about the author and purpose of every document, but about its intended audience. Why was the document produced, and what effect was it supposed to have? What does it tell you about the time, the place, the people?

Secondary sources. Typically, a secondary source is a book or article that reflects on and interprets a primary source. Secondary works range from scholarly works by professional historians to journalistic accounts. Just as we are shaped by our environments and the events of our own times, so secondary works vary depending on the place and time in which they were written. For example, the growth of activist feminism in the later 1960s and the 1970s led to an expansion of women's history, and, more recently, some important land claims disputes have refocused historians' attention on Canada's Aboriginal peoples. Every secondary work must be evaluated on its own merits, particularly on how well it uses primary sources as evidence; but as a general rule, you should always look for the most up-to-date work you can find.

In some cases the distinction between primary sources and secondary works may be confusing. If you are writing about historical writers, for instance, you may find yourself using a secondary work as a primary source. In the 1880s and 1890s, for example, an English-born Canadian named William Kingsford wrote a 10-volume *History of Canada* that celebrated the new Dominion as the triumph of British values. Since it tells us as much about the attitudes of middle-class Anglophones in Kingsford's day as it does about the events leading up to Confederation, Kingsford's work could be used as a primary source for a study of Canada in the late nineteenth century.

Distinguish Scholarly from Popular History

Not everyone who writes history is a trained historian. Professional historians and history professors undergo many years of study as well as rigorous training in the standards of evidence and accuracy. How can you tell a scholarly source from popular history?

Scholarly history. Scholarly books have gone through rigorous editing and peer review (check the acknowledgements page to see whether reviewers are mentioned) and often assume that their readers will have some background in the field. Most scholarly history is based on original research and is designed to inform rather than entertain. There will be plenty of footnotes, so that you can evaluate their evidence for yourself if you wish, and a full, detailed bibliography. Unless the subject is art history, such works typically have few, if any, illustrations or photographs, although they may well include charts, graphs, and other analytical images. Look also particularly for books published by university or other presses that concentrate

> **TIP!** Give yourself plenty of time for scholarly reading, and keep a dictionary handy!

on academic work (for confirmation, check the publisher's website). Stanley's work, mentioned above, is a scholarly source.

Historians also write scholarly articles, sometimes in the preliminary stages of research for an eventual book and sometimes simply on topics that interest them. For students, one advantage of articles is that they are short. More important, though, an article can usually be researched, written, and published far more quickly than a book: therefore articles tend to reflect both the latest thinking on a given subject and the most current methodology. For example, devastating windstorms in 2006 and 2007 that destroyed much of Vancouver's Stanley Park inspired the historian Sean Kheraj to find out more about the history of the park. The result was his article "Restoring Nature: Ecology, Memory and the Storm History of Vancouver's Stanley Park," published in the December 2007 edition of the *Canadian Historical Review*. This was followed in 2013 by *Inventing Stanley Park: An Environmental History*,[14] published by the University of British Columbia Press.

Look for articles in journals published either by academic institutions or by organizations such as the Champlain Society (which is devoted to preserving Canada's documentary heritage) or the Canadian Historical Association. These journals generally list an editorial board made up mainly of academics, and refer articles to peer reviewers before accepting them for publication. Look for a statement in the first few pages of the journal telling potential authors how to submit articles for publishing. These statements will generally say something about peer review before publication. Academic journals contain little or no advertising and are usually published quarterly. You will usually find these journals only in libraries, particularly academic libraries, and you will often find back issues shelved together in annual bound volumes. The *Canadian Historical Review*, *BC Studies*, and *Past and Present* are all examples of scholarly periodicals, as is the *Canadian Journal of Native Studies*, mentioned above. Note that your library's electronic catalogue may tell you in its article listing whether the article comes from a peer-reviewed journal. Your library system may also allow you to limit your article search to scholarly publications with peer review.

Popular history. In contrast, history written by people not necessarily specifically trained in history, such as journalists, is generally classified as popular. Such books often contain many photographs and they are usually designed to interest, or even entertain, non-scholarly readers as much as to inform them. They are not likely to have undergone peer review, and they generally do not include many references. Although it does not have extensive photographs, the Asfar and Chodan book, which lacks references and has an extremely brief bibliography, is typical.

The magazines you see on newsstands are usually non-scholarly. They typically have striking colour pictures on the front cover, are produced on glossy paper, and contain a lot of advertising and photographs. They are usually published weekly or monthly, their articles may be anonymous or written by staff reporters, and they will rarely have references or bibliographies. *Maclean's* is a typical popular magazine.

None of this is to say that all academic history is excellent and all popular history is second-rate. It is also only fair to point out that some academic historians also publish popular history and that some amateur historians produce work of very high quality. For example, Professor H.V. Nelles, who is a well-known academic historian, wrote *A Little History of Canada*[15] specifically for non-specialists, and Heather Robertson, a professional writer who did not train as a historian, published *Measuring Mother Earth*, an interesting account of Joseph Burr Tyrell, the nineteenth-century surveyor, explorer, and adventurer who discovered the first dinosaur skull in Canada.[16] Some newsstand magazines straddle the line between popular and academic: *Canada's History* (formerly known as *The Beaver*), *History Today*, and *Archaeology* often publish articles written by professionals. So do exercise your judgment when assessing sources, and don't automatically discount popular history. Just check with your professor whenever you aren't sure about the suitability of your source.

> **TIP!** A book that would look good on your coffee table is probably not a scholarly text!

Form a Hypothesis

Naturally, the goal of any researcher is to discover something new. This is a challenging proposition for a student, and by now you may be doubting your choice of topic. Stanley, Goulet, and a massive host of others have already written plenty about Riel. What new perspective can you bring to bear on the subject?

One of the most important steps in writing a research paper is to form a **hypothesis**: a question or proposition that will serve as a guide as you work your way through your source materials. As you read through the sources you will look for answers to your question, and as you find more answers you will gradually refine your hypothesis. Over the course of the research process, you will find that you are getting closer to forming an argument.

How do you arrive at a hypothesis? One way to begin is to jot down some questions. For example: (1) What sort of person was Riel? (2) What led Riel to become so politically and militarily active in the 1870s and 1880s? (3) How did he twice become the leader of resistance against Canadian expansion into the Northwest? (4) Why was the resistance somewhat successful in 1870, but such a failure in 1885? (5) Since he was not only possibly insane but also an American citizen, why was he executed for treason against Canada?

Now ask yourself two questions. First, if you are able to arrive at an answer to one of those questions, can you build an argument around it? Second, does the question address some broader issue in history? Questions 1 and 3 might yield only descriptions, not arguments. Questions 2 and 4 seem a bit more promising: they could lead, for example, into an analysis of the growth of Canadian political activism or of the development of federal–provincial relations. Question 5 also offers interesting possibilities for discussion of legal standards. Was the trial fair? Was it even legal? The answers to these types of questions could lead you to ask some broader questions about the social, cultural and political world of Post-Confederation Canada in which Riel moved and against which he struggled. Political power, its uses and abuses, are of considerable interest to many historians.

Draft a Proposal

After you have completed your preliminary research, draft a short proposal. Your teachers and friends may be willing to read it and comment on it. Even if they aren't, the process of writing the proposal will still help you to sketch out your ideas. The proposal is an early opportunity to think critically about your topic.

Every proposal should answer these questions:

1. What is your topic area? Describe it briefly.
2. What is the hypothesis that will drive your research?
3. What will your readers learn from this project? Will you be bringing new information to light, or interpreting commonplace knowledge in a new way?
4. Why is your project significant or interesting? Discuss the relationship between your project and some broader issue in history.
5. What are your principal sources? Give a short bibliography.
6. What are your source materials? Will you be relying on library books? Exploring **archival materials**? Analyzing objects or paintings? What methods will you use? Are any of your sources in a foreign or specialized technical language? If so, can you understand them? Will you be using methods from another discipline, such as sociology?

> **TIP!** Now's a good time to talk with your professor about your project—you may get some helpful advice!

Write an Annotated Bibliography

The next step is to compile an **annotated bibliography**. This exercise will help you assess the breadth and significance of the sources you have found. List your references according to the instructions for creating a bibliography in Chapter 5 below. Now, after each entry, briefly describe the work and explain how you will be using it in your paper. Describe any special circumstances surrounding the source. For example, is it an eyewitness account? Might its author have a specific bias or some particular technical expertise? In general, these remarks should be concise, but you may say more about some sources than others.

An annotated bibliography on the trial of Louis Riel might contain the following entries:

Flanagan, Thomas. *Riel and the Rebellion: 1885 Reconsidered.* 2nd rev. ed. Toronto: University of Toronto Press, 2000. Flanagan is not sympathetic to Riel. Admits that the Canadian government made some mistakes, but argues they'd taken care of all the real grievances of the Metis, who didn't really use or need the land properly anyway. Flanagan paints Riel as an outside agitator and a fanatic who really was just interfering in Northwest life and affairs and who misrepresented Canadian government actions to the Metis.

Goulet, George R.D. *The Trial of Louis Riel: Justice and Mercy Denied.* 3rd ed. Calgary: Tellwell Publishing, 2005. Goulet is a retired lawyer and a descendant of one of Riel's followers. He argues that the trial was essentially rigged and was not even legal. He says the judge was biased, Riel's defence was incompetent and his rights denied. He also argues that the court had no legal jurisdiction because the old English law on treason was not applicable.

Groarke, Paul. "The Trial and Execution of Louis Riel: Defending my Country the Northwest." *Canadian Journal of Native Studies.* July 2013, Vol.33, issue 2, 1–28. Groarke agrees with Goulet on all the points above. Says insanity was the only defence Riel's lawyers argued, but Riel himself also raised two others: Canadian Crown had no right to the territory; Metis had a right and a duty to defend themselves against the Canadian invaders. Riel not willing to go with the insanity thing, which the Crown denied anyway, and ended up having to argue *against* his lawyers and *for* his own conviction.

Mumford, Jeremy Ravi. "Why Was Louis Riel, a United States Citizen, Hanged as a Canadian Traitor in 1885?" *Canadian Historical Review.* Vol.88. Issue 2. 2007. 237–62. Mumford asks how Riel could count as a traitor when he'd legally and formally renounced his allegiance to the Queen, and why the United States didn't try to protect him, as they'd been doing for other political militants. Answer in two directions. 1. Neither Riel nor his lawyers pushed the citizenship question as they might have done. 2. US internal political situation in 1885 got in the way of action. Mumford also argues that we think of Riel as Canadian, but he was really the "leader of the Metis, distinct from any nation-state" (261). The border didn't have much meaning for the Metis. Note: good bibliographical sources in this article.

Stanley, George F.G. *Louis Riel.* Toronto: Ryerson Press, 1963. Stanley was a long-time Canadian history professor, and he says in his preface (no page number) that this should be "an authoritative life of Louis Riel." Nearly all the later writers mention this book, so it still seems to be influential.

The Queen v. Louis Riel. Desmond Morton intro. The Social History of Canada. Toronto: U of T. Press, 1974. Mostly a primary source: the complete transcript of the trial. Morton's intro gives an overview of events from the time of Riel's capture to his execution, then a brief analysis. Morton says Riel "was essentially guilty as charged" (xxix) and accepts that he was insane, but possibly not "by the standards of his own day" (xxix).

> **TIP!** You can use annotated bibliographies both to record info about the sources and also to make notes to yourself.

Notice that the *Queen v. Louis Riel* is a book from a series called The Social History of Canada. You will need this information for your paper's bibliography. Note also that this entry includes a direct quotation. Always be sure to note quotations with quotation marks, and record their sources: doing this as you go along will save you many tedious hours checking sources later. Also record which parts of your notes are direct paraphrases, and note the relevant page numbers.

Talk about Your Topic

Don't be bashful. Talk about your topic with other people: friends, relatives, teachers, even specialists in the field. If you were researching longitude, for instance, you might seek out a specialist in geography or astronomy, or try to find some navigational equipment and ask an expert to show you how to use it. Experts are usually happy to discuss specific research questions, especially if the questions are thoughtful. If the experts happen to teach at your university, you may be able to visit them during their office hours; if not, make appointments to see them and consider submitting your question(s) in writing, some time in advance.

If You Have to Abandon a Topic, Do it Early

Finding sources, forming a hypothesis, and drafting a proposal will test the viability of your project. It's possible that, at the end of that process, you will decide that you haven't found enough sources, or that the topic is less interesting than you had expected, or that your research has led you to a different, more promising topic area. If the project isn't working, it's better to bail out of it early than to go down in flames later. But you will need time to start over. Of course, this means that you should begin working on any project as soon as possible.

REVIEW

1. Find a topic that interests you.
2. Mine your library for print and online sources.
3. Read bibliographies to find more sources.
4. Make sure your sources are appropriate.
5. Read to develop a hypothesis and craft a proposal.
6. Take careful notes, showing quotations and paraphrases.

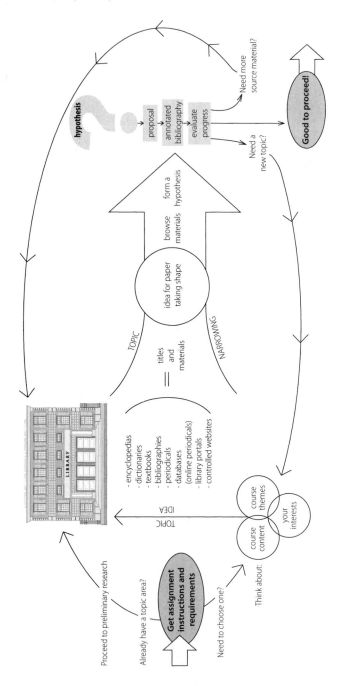

Using and Interpreting Source Materials

At first you may find that your sources seem confusing or even contradictory. An important part of writing history is deciding how to interpret and assemble material from sources that may raise more questions than they answer. Some sources will lead historians on an exhilarating chase that culminates in a dead end. Others will make it possible to recover unexpected tales from the past. Fortunately, there are many ways of interpreting source materials.

> **TIP!** Think as you read!

Ask the Reporter's Questions

Richard Marius was a historian who began his career as a journalist. In his *Short Guide to Writing about History*, he advises students to approach source materials the same way reporters approach stories: by asking five basic questions.[17] It's good advice.

Suppose that you're writing an essay on Louis Riel and your sources consist mainly of nineteenth-century archival materials such as newspaper reports, government documents, and personal memoirs. Your hypothesis questions whether Riel's militancy represented the majority political view on the South Saskatchewan River in 1884–5. As you read about Riel's decisions, consider organizing your research around the reporter's questions. When you start to get answers, take notes and use them to help you develop ideas for your essay.

"Who" questions. Historians ask "who" to learn biographical information about significant actors and to find out who caused things to happen and who bore the brunt of historical changes. In the case

of Riel, you could use "who" questions to acquaint yourself with the various characters involved. What groups made up the South Saskatchewan community? Who actively supported Riel? Who actively opposed him? Who remained on the fringes?

"What" questions. Different sources often describe the same events differently. Know each version of events so that you can compare accounts. Suppose you are focusing on Riel's decision to return to the Northwest in 1884. What did he understand of the situation there after living in the United States for some years? What did he know of the population and the wider political realities? What did he do to find out about the situation? What did he do to gain support for his decisions and actions? What were the strategic and political consequences of his return?

"Why" questions. Why did some things change while others remained the same? Using each source, make a list of possible causes of events. Try to distinguish the most significant causes from the background causes. Why was Riel successful in his 1870 rebellion but not in 1885? Did the answer lie in himself, in others, or in the changed circumstances? Was his leadership less effective in 1885? Had he himself changed? Was the level or the quality of community different? Was the response from the federal government different?

"Where" questions. In some cases you will find fairly self-evident answers to "where" questions. In others geographical considerations will open your eyes to unexpected circumstances. You might even find it helpful to draw a map of your subject. Where, for example, is Batoche? Was this a wise choice for his headquarters? Might a stronger stand have been made elsewhere? Might a different location have affected the level or quality of the support he received? What was the route of the new railway? Did this route make a difference to the outcome of events?

"When" questions. Historians analyze change and continuity over time. Not surprisingly, it's important to know when historical events

happened. Depending on the topic, you may get an easy answer, a complex one, or no answer at all. Do your best to determine when things happened. Then use this information to place events in a chronological relationship. Try to make one timeline from all your source materials so that you can see the order of events. When, for example, did Riel decide to move from petitions and diplomatic appeals to armed resistance? If he had made this decision earlier, might the outcome have been different? Would the federal government have been able to send troops just as quickly?

"How" questions. Marius did not include "how" questions in his list, but they are also helpful to think about. In the case of Riel, you might want to ask how events played out and how they fit into a wider context. How did Riel and local Metis leaders relate to one another? How did the press in Ontario and Quebec react to the news of the events on the South Saskatchewan? How were political decisions and actions in Ottawa affected by Riel's activities? How did the arrival of the railway influence the decisions of the politicians? How did the Riel affair affect the delicate balance between Ontario and Quebec? How did it affect the development of Quebec nationalism?

You will not always find answers to every question you come up with, and should not be distressed about this. Asking the questions and searching the evidence to try to answer them helps you to think about the material and what it means. Notice also that some questions naturally lead to others—for example, the "when" question above leads immediately into a more speculative and analytical consideration about results.

Be Sensitive to Points of View

As you use your hypothesis to work through the source materials, you will come to see that many sources present history from a particular point of view. Even photographs show only the perspective of the photographer. Photographers have been known to pose or arrange their subjects sometimes even for what look like action shots, and the mere presence of a camera often changes the way people behave. How do you know which sources to trust? Historians must be sensitive to the fact that those who record events as they happen are likely to describe only the events they consider interesting or important.

Similarly, participants are likely to describe events from their own point of view. In her article "To See Ourselves as the Other's Other: Nlaka'pamux Contact Narratives," Wendy Wickwire discusses the explorer Simon Fraser's encounters with the Nlaka'pamux people of south-central British Columbia. Using both Fraser's journal (the more widely known historical source) and Nlaka'pamux oral history, Wickwire finds many similarities between the two accounts, but also some differences. One of the most striking differences concerns Fraser's encounter with a young woman, an encounter that is not mentioned in the diary but is presented as a highly significant event in the oral account. In this case, each account focused on the concerns of the participants and was created from that perspective alone. A similar point can be made about all contemporary sources: a chronicler's decisions on what to record generally reflect a combination of personal and community perspectives on what is important and what is not—or, sometimes, what one ought to keep silent about.[18]

The creation of source materials does not end with the choices made by the chroniclers. All sorts of factors determine whether or not a chronicle will survive and be accessible. Sometimes records are destroyed by fire, flood, or war. Often governments, collectors, archivists, and librarians decide to preserve some records and discard or even deliberately destroy others. They have their own visions of the past, and politics and economics can influence their decisions in many ways.

During the 1960s, a distinguished historian of science named Loren Graham began to collect information about a Soviet engineer named Peter Palchinsky, who was executed by Stalin in 1929. Graham believed that Palchinsky had made significant contributions to early Soviet engineering, but that the Soviet government was hiding his papers because

> **TIP!** Keep your eyes critical and mind open when reading your sources.

he had criticized the regime. Graham had to wait almost 30 years, but he finally gained access to Palchinsky's papers after the collapse of the Soviet Union. Then, in a nice twist of fate, he found that the Palchinsky papers shed light on the failure of the Soviet system. His quest for sources became a subplot of his history, *The Ghost of the Executed Engineer.*[19] But even in Graham's case, the choices made by the chroniclers influenced the writing of history.

Select the Most Important Information

If you want to make an argument, it's not enough just to collect facts; you have to select the relevant ones and arrange them in a suitable structure. You can't include everything in your essay. You must choose the information you need to make your point, even if that means ignoring some interesting tangents or anecdotes.

In the course of your research, you will find some information that is directly relevant to your essay and much that is not. Don't feel bad if you've spent a lot of time investigating a source, only to find that it doesn't contribute to your essay's main idea. If you are tempted to include such material anyway, because it is interesting or even just to show your readers how hard you have worked, resist the temptation. Readers will be much more impressed by a coherent essay in which all the content is clearly relevant to the main point.

Take Notes Selectively

You should start taking notes as soon as you begin to analyze your sources. The method you choose for taking notes will depend in part on the type of research you are conducting and in part on your personal preference. As you do more research, you will get a better sense of how you like to work.

Some historians use notebooks or index cards; others use word-processing or database programs. Online citation management systems such as Zotero (for PCs and Macs) or Citavi (for PCs only), both easily available online, can be helpful for students. These programs allow you to download references directly to your own computer.

They keep records of your sources and arrange these records into lists formatted in the style you prefer (although it is always a good idea to check that they've got it right!). The programs' capabilities vary. Some allow you to download quotations or even whole articles, some let you add your own notes, and some record your searches so that you

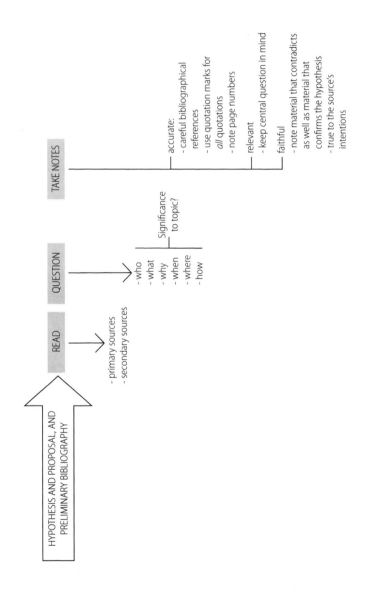

can later go back to find something that you did not originally see as relevant. Your academic library website may well have information on citation management systems, and some institutions specifically support one or more of the systems, so do check for this. In addition, for many citation management systems it is easy to find online tutorials.

Much more important than the way you take notes is what they contain. You will save yourself a lot of time and effort later if you start each note with all of the publication information, including author and publisher, and date and place of publication. If your book or article has a title and subtitle, record both. In the case of a journal article, be sure to record the issue number and the total pages of the article. In most cases, unless the original words are particularly striking, you don't want to copy your sources word for word. You want to write down only the information that is likely to be useful in your essay. But how do you know what is going to be useful before you begin to write? Making these decisions is the most difficult part of note-taking. You don't want to write down useless information, but you recognize that some irrelevant-looking information may turn out to be useful later on.

It's difficult to know in advance which notes will be useful. This is why you should use your hypothesis to help you read sources. Ask yourself how each source relates to your hypothesis, and jot down notes from the source that answer fundamental questions about your hypothesis. Use your hypothesis to help select the most important information from your sources.

The trickiest thing at this stage is that your hypothesis is likely to change. This is as it should be. Over the course of your research, as you learn more about your subject, your ideas about it will become clearer and you will be able

> **TIP!** Remember to show clearly in your notes if you are quoting or paraphrasing.

to refine your hypothesis to the point where it can become a **thesis** or argument. Unfortunately, this means that some of your early notes will be more extensive and less useful than your later notes. Don't be disappointed if, at the end of a project, you find that you've taken some notes that you didn't use and needed to return to your earlier sources to check material that did not originally seem important to record: this is a natural consequence of the process of selection and refinement.

Work Systematically

Historians do not make random choices. They work as systematically as possible, selecting their evidence according to rules that they share with writers across the disciplines. Hippocrates' advice to ancient Greek doctors might well apply to today's historians:

> In Medicine one must pay attention not to plausible theorizing but to experience and reason together. . . . I agree that theorizing is to be approved, provided that it is based on facts, and systematically makes its deductions from what is observed. . . . But conclusions drawn by the unaided reason can hardly be serviceable; only those drawn from observed facts.[20]

Like Hippocrates, historians do theorize, and they must do so. Sometimes, evidence such as primary source material is scarce, or even non-existent, and this in itself forces them to come up with theories. However, historians must think carefully to decide how far to theorize and what are reasonable conclusions. They always try to take all the available evidence into account when theorizing, and also use their common sense and experience of the world. For example, while we do not have much objective evidence to explain how the Egyptian pyramids were built, and indeed many theories have been suggested, respectable historians reject any idea of space aliens being involved. Arguments need to be reasonable and based as far as possible in evidence, and theories need to make sense in view of this evidence. So how do historians work with their source materials?

It is impossible to know exactly what happened in the past, but that has not stopped people from writing about it. The American poet Walt Whitman (1819–92) wrote that the "interior history" of his country's Civil War "will not only never be written—its practicality, minutiae of deeds and passions, will never be even suggested."[21] That may be true, but it did not stop Whitman from trying to interpret the war by making reasoned inferences from sources. An **inference** is more than a hunch. It is an intelligent conclusion reached through examination and comparison of evidence. After visiting a number of wounded soldiers in an army hospital, Whitman concluded that the war was indescribably brutal. When he put his conclusion in writing, people believed him even though he had not seen every casualty or every battlefield. He had seen enough wounded men to build his inference into a persuasive argument. Like Whitman, historians arrive at probable interpretations by using their sources to make inferences.

What is it that makes an inferential argument interesting? Good writers make inferences by juxtaposing sources in a new, provocative way. At a time when people on both sides, North and South, were mobilizing armies to kill and maim one another, Whitman recognized that it would take more than pacifist principles to turn public opinion against the war. It would take evidence, built by inferences into an argument, to change the way that people thought. New evidence, or a new approach to old evidence, called into question the received wisdom of the day.

Inferential reasoning is based on thoughtful comparison. When modern-day historians write about the past, they try never to rely on a single source: they cross-check the information provided by various sources. Even when there is only one source on a given subject, they will assess it in the light of their own general knowledge, look for points of comparison with other works, and use those works to put their material into a wider context.

About Facts

Every inference begins with careful consideration of the facts. Determining what the facts are is a large part of a historian's job, of course. But there is no need to start back at square one every time: many facts are easy to recognize and should be taken as given.

Occasionally you may encounter people who are overly skeptical about recognized facts. For example, some people deny that the

Holocaust ever happened, despite the millions who experienced, witnessed, and documented it.[22] One organization of polemicists posing as historians even has its own journal dedicated to "proving" its point. Real historical writers investigate factual uncertainties, but they do not invent convenient facts and they don't ignore inconvenient ones. People are entitled to their own opinions—not to their own facts.

> **TIP!** Don't be so committed to your own idea that you ignore other points of view—deal with them fairly and openly. If you can't deal with them, then think hard: is your hypothesis sustainable?

Transform Facts into Evidence

There is more to writing history than simply gathering facts and arranging them in some sort of order. In itself, the existence of a fact doesn't prove anything. Facts gain meaning only when we examine and interpret them. As Professor John H. Arnold remarks, historians try to create an interesting, coherent and useful narrative about the past. The past itself is not a narrative. In its entirety, it is as chaotic, uncoordinated, and complex as life. History is about making sense of that mess, finding or creating patterns and meanings and stories from the maelstrom.[23] Historians seek out the most reliable information and do their best to establish its accuracy before they use it to make inferences.

Check Your Facts

It's not always easy to tell where "the facts" stop and the interpretation begins. In Canada, for instance, the 1990s were a period of intense debate on the rights of First Nations. The historical geographer Cole Harris, recognizing that the size of pre-contact indigenous populations in British Columbia could have some bearing on issues such as land claims, also recognized that both Aboriginal and non-Aboriginal estimates could be influenced by political and economic considerations. Therefore he set out to determine accurate figures. He did not simply accept the claims of either "side," and he did not accept that it was impossible so many years later to determine the population size. Instead,

Harris gathered all the data he could find, examining the oral history traditions of the peoples concerned as well as the written accounts of Europeans and the work of earlier ethnographers. Harris published his research in the first chapter of *The Resettlement of British Columbia*. He concluded that the pre-contact population was probably over 200,000, possibly over 400,000, and that it had been decimated by "European" diseases even before direct contact with Europeans.[24] Follow Cole Harris's example and take an informed but pragmatic approach to facts. Very often, facts will be self-evident, but sometimes historians find that supposed facts rest on nothing more than assumptions and preconceptions. There are several procedures that can help in determining the truth of questionable "facts."

About Sources

Check the Internal Consistency of All Sources

If a source contradicts itself, there is probably a discernible reason. For example, the richest sources of information on rural north China during the Japanese occupation are the reports written between 1940 and 1942 by teams of sociologists who were sent by the Japanese government's South Manchurian Railway Company to interview large numbers of peasants. These reports contain many contradictions, for the peasants (not surprisingly) mistrusted the occupiers and sometimes lied to them.

Nevertheless, several historians have used the interviews as sources of information on the economy, society, and politics of the region.[25] They have done so using internal inferences—obtained by comparing the statements of individual peasants on specific issues—and then checking them against other sources of information on rural north China.

All sources have been subject to some biases in creation and selection, but that does not mean that historians cannot try to determine what happened.

Check Primary Sources against One Another

Comparing source materials can lead to important new inferences. One such breakthrough involved the well-known life of Louis Pasteur, who made some of the most significant contributions to nineteenth-century biology. After Pasteur died in 1895, the accounts of his life published by colleagues and family were uniformly admiring. Historians knew that they should be skeptical of such sources, but they had no evidence to the contrary until 1938, when Pasteur's nephew and laboratory assistant, Adrien Loir, claimed that the great doctor had misled the judges at the public trials of his anthrax vaccine. Because historians had no evidence to substantiate Loir's claim, however, the heroic myth remained in place until the 1970s, when Pasteur's laboratory notebooks passed out of his family to the French state. When the historian Gerald Geison gained access to them, he found that they confirmed Loir's account. Using the notebooks to re-evaluate Pasteur's experimental practices, Geison moved Loir's account from the background to the foreground and wrote an important book entitled *The Private Science of Louis Pasteur*.[26]

Compare Primary and Secondary Sources

Historical knowledge changes incrementally as new information alters historians' understanding of, and sometimes access to, the past. When new materials or methods become available, historians often find themselves using primary sources to refine or contradict the ideas proposed by earlier secondary works. One famous recent example comes from British history and connects directly with Canada.

Historian and genealogist John Ashdown-Hill had become interested in England's controversial King Richard III, who was killed in battle in 1485. According to the earliest accounts, Richard's mutilated body had been buried without ceremony in an abbey church in Leicester, and the exact location had been forgotten almost immediately. A rival family now held the English throne, and it was in their interests to portray Richard negatively. William Shakespeare obligingly wrote the play *Richard III*, portraying Richard as a hunchbacked, child-killing monster. Richard went into history as a villain, and many (although not all) historians simply accepted and repeated that point of view. Professional genealogist Ashdown-Hill, who is also a member of a society dedicated to rehabilitating Richard's reputation, used his expertise to track down a Canadian descendant from Richard's family and establish what would be Richard's mitochondrial DNA sequence. In 2013, when archaeologists did unexpectedly find an ancient skeleton buried under what was now a parking lot, it was thus possible to identify it specifically as Richard, to study it in detail and establish that his spine was indeed physically malformed, although he would not have been hunchbacked, The discovery and identification of Richard III's body is a good illustration of one way in which modern science can be relevant for historians. Using the primary source of Richard's body we are now able to dismiss the hunchback idea, and several historians have been inspired to take another look at the accounts of his life and his death.[27] This has opened up a whole set of new directions for study and also inspired historians to take another, more open-minded, look at Richard and to what extent he deserved his negative reputation.

Juxtapose Sources

In the course of your research and writing, you will need to check both primary and secondary sources for internal consistency. You will also need to compare primary sources and secondary works against one another. How does the process of comparison work in practice?

In the 1970s, the historian Robin Fisher studied the effects of contact with Europeans on the First Nations of the Pacific coast. Up to that point, historians had taken little notice of the indigenous peoples of the region that would become British Columbia, but the general view was that their societies had been devastated by the arrival of Europeans on the coast in the late 1700s. Fisher looked at the work of earlier historians and anthropologists. He also read carefully the records and diaries of Spanish, American, and British explorers and traders such as Juan Pérez, Robert Haswell, and James Cook.

Comparing these documents, he found that the First Nations' part in the maritime fur trade had been ignored, and that the effect of the trade on their societies had been misunderstood, in part because of scholars' preconceptions and assumptions. In his seminal book *Contact and Conflict*, Fisher concluded that the peoples of the Pacific coast were sophisticated traders who knew very well how to get what they wanted and were able to set the terms of trade with the

Europeans.[28] According to Fisher, the devastation of Native societies came later, as a result of White settlement. Not all historians and anthropologists accepted Fisher's argument either then or now, but by using a variety of sources, looking at them with new eyes, and drawing his own conclusions, Fisher sparked an interest in the history of British Columbian Aboriginal peoples that continues to the present.

> **TIP!** Good research does not always come up with the "right" answer—in fact there may well not be a right answer. Good research is firmly based in evidence and it advances knowledge and inspires ideas.

About Inferences and Arguments

Making inferences allows historians to say something new. This can be an intimidating proposition, especially if you are a beginning student or working on a topic that has already been studied by many scholars. But judging by the contents of most bookstores, historians are always finding something new to say about old topics. Just when you think the Second World War has been studied to death, a new book appears.

There are many ways to say something new. Experienced historians know that new ideas come out of close and careful comparisons of primary and secondary sources. A new idea in one field can shed light on an old source; the discovery of a new source can inspire historians to rethink some old ideas. In fact, every historian brings a unique personal perspective to all sources.

> **TIP!** Think! What does your evidence tell you? What does it not tell you? Can you find more information to fill the gap?

Still, novelty for its own sake is pointless. Small inferences must be built into larger arguments, and arguments must be made persuasively. As you read your sources, start thinking about ways to construct your essay. How can you move from

Make Inferences from Material Sources

Most of the source materials used by academic writers are written documents. However, historians of science and technology, archaeologists, and art historians, among others, frequently analyze material objects. Learning to analyze objects can give you new perspectives, but it takes practice. Among the most common methods used by writers across the disciplines to analyze material evidence are the following (based on an article by Jules Prown called "Mind in Matter"):

1. **Describe the object.** What can you observe about the object itself? Give a physical description. How is the object shaped? If you can measure it, what are its dimensions (size, weight)? If you can't measure it, estimate the dimensions. Can you see any obvious symbols on the object, such as markings, decorations, or inscriptions?
2. **Think about the object.** At this very moment, what is it like to interact with the object? What does the object feel like? When you use it, do you have to take into account its size, weight, or shape? What does the object do, and how? Does it work well? What is it like to use it? How do you feel about using this object? Do you like it? Does it frustrate you? Is it puzzling?
3. **Make an argument about the object.** Can you analyze the object imaginatively and plausibly? Review your descriptions and **deductions**. What sorts of hypotheses can you propose about the object? Can you make a historically significant argument about it? What might it have been like for someone to use this object in the past? Use other sources as a lens for interpreting the object. What other evidence can you use to test your hypotheses, speculations, and deductions?[29]

asking questions about events and sources to composing a story and developing an argument of your own? This is the most challenging aspect to writing any history. You must consider the arguments of your primary sources and secondary works, then engage them constructively and responsibly.

Make Reasonable Inferences from Your Sources

Source materials impose healthy constraints on historical writers. You may have a hunch that English maritime explorers landed in

North America before the time of Christopher Columbus, but after careful review of primary sources and secondary works, you will find no evidence to support your hypothesis. Don't worry. You thought that you could make a breathtakingly novel argument, but it is much more important that you recognize the limits of your sources. Don't expect too much from your sources, and don't read into them what you hope to find. Sometimes you may even be able to write an essay about how little you can learn from the sources on a particular subject. Even so, if you cannot use a source to support your argument, you must be prepared either to redefine your questions or move on to another set of sources.

Make Inferences That Are Warranted

How do historians know a good inference from a bad one? Under what circumstances are inferences warranted?

The ancient Greeks divided arguments from inferences into two categories: **deduction** and **induction**. When you are reading and writing history, use the categories of deduction and induction to help you decide which arguments from inferences are warranted.

Deductive reasoning. In deductive reasoning, a writer makes an inference based on a limited amount of evidence, but the inference is trustworthy because it is consistent with conventional wisdom. In other words, deduction means applying general rules to particular circumstances.

Here is an example of a historical deduction: "The gaps in the Watergate tapes must mean that (US President Richard) Nixon had something to hide." What sort of evidence do historians have to support this statement? The Watergate tapes do contain large gaps, but Nixon never admitted to hiding anything. The White House blamed the gaps on the president's secretary, saying that she had accidentally erased portions of the tapes. Why did most people not believe this? Common sense indicated that the missing passages had contained evidence that would incriminate Nixon, that he had a motive for erasing them, and that he also had the access necessary to do so.

Break this argument down into its deductive components and this is what it looks like:

- Evidence: The Watergate tapes contain large gaps.
- Common-sense proposition: The official explanation is less credible than the idea that the tapes were erased to destroy evidence against the president.
- Inference: The fact that the tapes delivered to investigators were incomplete means that Nixon was hiding something.

Although writers rarely state their reasoning in such a schematic way, common-sense deductions often provide the bases for inferences based on limited information.

On the other hand, common sense can be deceptive. It is possible to challenge the inferences of historical writers by testing whether their deductions really are based on common sense. All historians have heard the story about how Columbus wanted to prove that the Earth was round and not flat. According to the legend, Columbus's contemporaries believed the Earth was flat because they had a weak common-sense basis:

- Evidence: The Earth appeared to be flat.
- Common-sense proposition: Humans can distinguish between flat objects and round objects.
- Inference: The Earth is flat, not round.

In fact, humans can't always distinguish flat objects from round objects, at least not on the planetary scale. If your common-sense idea is weak, then there must be a flaw in your reasoning. Take care to test your assumptions especially if they are unstated. If you don't test them yourself, your readers certainly will.

Inductive reasoning. Inductive reasoning is often associated with science. This is because inductive reasoning begins with many pieces of evidence and generalizes from them. Induction operates on the warrant that a conclusion based on a large quantity of data is likely to be correct. Take the following statement: "Statistics Canada data suggest that in 2008, women in Canada who had less than a grade-9 education and who worked full-time earned less money than men with comparable education levels. The gap decreased, but was still statistically significant at higher educational levels." What are the components of this inductive statement?

- Evidence: Statistics Canada data show that in 2008 there were significant gaps between the incomes of educationally comparable men and women.
- Inductive concept: If you have plenty of data pointing to the same conclusion, that conclusion is likely correct.
- Inference: Based on the evidence, Canadian women would be more likely than men to suffer economic hardship.

The most common way to test such an inference is to question whether the evidence is sufficient to support the conclusion. The inductive concept is difficult to challenge.

Avoid Unwarranted Comparisons

To write history is to speak on behalf of people who lived in the past. This is a tremendous responsibility, and it is the reason historians are cautious about comparisons. Some comparisons allow historians to make strong inferences about the past; others are pointless or even irresponsible. In a study of the conflict among German historians over how Nazism and the Holocaust should be interpreted, Charles Maier makes the point that some historical comparisons are "licit" and some are not. He criticizes those historians who compare the Holocaust to other genocides for the inappropriate purpose of alleviating German guilt.[30]

A reasonable comparison can be found in John Mack Farragher's account of the British expulsion of the Acadians from their colonial territories in the 1750s. Farragher suggests that this action "was the first episode of state-sponsored ethnic cleansing in North American history."[31] To make the comparison, Farragher juxtaposes the expulsion of the Acadians with twentieth-century episodes of forced migration or ethnic cleansing and demonstrates that the events in Acadia matched the 1992 UN Commission of Experts' definition of the latter. Although the term "ethnic cleansing" was unknown in the eighteenth century, Farragher establishes that the expulsion was comparable to modern events both in its purpose and in its consequences for the Acadians.

Avoid Anachronistic Inferences

Although modern-day comparisons can shed valuable light on historical events, you should never place your subjects in situations that they would not recognize.

Some anachronisms are easy to avoid. No one would suggest Caesar glanced at his wristwatch before crossing the Rubicon. Other types of anachronism may not be so obvious, however. For example, the French historian Georges Lefebvre wanted to use Marxist theory to explain the origins of the French Revolution. But when Lefebvre wrote his book *The Coming of the French Revolution*, he knew he could not argue that the French working classes intended to form a communist party and establish a dictatorship of the proletariat. Such an anachronistic claim would not have been true to the experience of eighteenth-century French people, who had never heard of such things as the Communist Party or the dictatorship of the proletariat. Instead, Lefebvre gained a heightened awareness of class conflict from reading Marx, then used this awareness to ask new questions of his sources.[32]

Many students get interested in history because they want to understand the origins of something in the present, but it's essential to recognize that people who lived in the past almost certainly had different perspectives on their activities than modern researchers do. For example, although some of the origins of modern physics are commonly traced to Sir Isaac Newton (1643–1727), Newton's own thinking was heavily influenced by alchemy and theology—areas of study that may well seem bizarre from a modern scientific perspective. As Betty Jo Teeter Dobbs suggests in her book *The Janus Faces of Genius*, to understand the role that alchemy played in Newton's thought, the historian must "reconstruct . . . the lens through which Newton viewed himself."[33] It is perfectly legitimate to ask contemporary questions about former times, but historians must remain faithful to the perspectives of the people who lived in those times.

REVIEW

1. Question your sources.
2. Be aware of sources' points of view, and of your own.
3. Be prepared to adjust your hypothesis as you go along.
4. Check facts carefully.
5. Compare evidence from a variety of sources.
6. Develop an argument based on all the evidence.
7. Be true to your characters' reality.

Continue to search out and read additional materials, check facts, compare sources and interpretations, refine ideas

THINK!

WHAT DOES IT ALL MEAN?

INFERENCES

YOUR THESIS

based on all the evidence

reflects the evidence fairly

comes from your own thinking

4

Get Writing!

After days, weeks, or months of gathering and analyzing information, the time will finally come when you have to start writing. The transition from research to writing is often the most difficult stage of any project. Scholars facing a blank screen should heed the advice of Samuel Eliot Morison, one of the greatest historians of navigation. In an article entitled "History as a Literary Art: An Appeal to Young Historians," Morison urged students to resist the temptation to hunt down that one last source or to brew just one more pot of coffee. Morison insisted that his students "First and foremost, *get writing!*"[34]

> **TIP!** Don't worry about anything yet except getting all your ideas down on paper.

Don't waste time wondering whether you have enough to say: if you have done your research thoroughly and really thought carefully about what you have learned, you will have plenty. And it doesn't matter if the writing is not perfect. You will find it much easier to correct mistakes in a draft than to come up with the material in the first place.

Narrative and Analysis

So how do you start? First you need to find a suitable framework for your argument.

By now you have read a variety of sources, all of which have added to your knowledge and helped you to adjust and refine your ideas. Now your hypothesis has become a thesis: the main point of the argument that you will sustain throughout your essay. You also know which pieces of evidence you will be using to support that argument. But you may not know yet how you want to organize the essay: as one long narrative that touches on analytical topics, or as an analysis that uses short narratives to illustrate specific points. A good way to decide this crucial question is to create two short outlines, one for each approach.

Draft Outline of an Analytical Essay

In the early stages of writing, it's usually helpful to create an outline that shows the broad lines of your argument, in order to test its feasibility.

Let's suppose that you have chosen to analyze the fairness and legality of Louis Riel's trial. This means that you are telling the story of the trial in order to examine an analytical problem. In that case your outline might look something like this:

I.   Introduction: The Northwest Rebellion and its causes; the role of Louis Riel; the role of the Canadian federal government
II. The trial's process
     A. Judge, lawyers, and jury
     B. Charges and main arguments
     C. Verdict and execution
III. The trial analyzed
     A. The choices of judge and jury members
     B. Riel's sanity
     C. Riel's citizenship status and the applicability of treason laws
IV. Conclusion
     A. The trial was neither entirely fair not entirely legal
     B. Significance of this story

This essay tells a single narrative and uses it to illustrate an analytical question: the extent to which the judicial process could be subverted to the needs and problems of the state.

Complete Analytical Outline

The draft outline above only provides a skeletal framework for an **analytical essay**. It may be useful as a beginning, but it doesn't do much to help you articulate your argument. To put some flesh on the bones, you need to add supporting points and details. The main point of the essay, the thesis, should be clearly stated in the introduction. The thesis statement sets up the whole paper, and everything that follows should be devoted to proving it. A complete outline of an analytical essay will show how you are moving from one analytical topic to another in order to accomplish this goal.

I.   Introduction: By the early 1880s, the constituent groups in the Northwest had serious grievances against the Canadian federal government. Decision by some to ask Louis Riel to lead a protest movement. Protest erupted into armed rebellion, which was defeated. Federal government response to the rebellion and in the later judicial process was determined by federal needs rather than by the specific issues in the Northwest. This illustrates how the judicial process could be subverted by the needs of the state:

   A.   The government wanted to fully establish its rule in the Northwest. Suppressing and fully discrediting the rebellion helped to accomplish this goal.

   B.   The rebellion and trial created strong feelings among the populations of Ontario and Quebec, and the government had to choose whom to appease.

II. The trial itself is worth examining.

   A.   The judge and Crown (= prosecution) lawyers were easterners, chosen by the federal government.

   B.   Riel was charged with violating a 1352 British treason statute. Prosecution argued he was instigator and leader of rebellion, that he'd asked for a money bribe to stop the action, and that he wanted to break up Canada. Defence argued, over LR's objections, that he was insane and therefore not criminally responsible.

C. Judge instructed jury on definition of insanity and reminded them about the bribe. Jury deliberated quickly, verdict of guilty but with plea for mercy in sentencing. Judge said death.

III. Analysis of trial suggests several issues of fairness and legality.

A. Judge was a federal political appointee, not in a permanent position, so was anxious to please Ottawa. Disliked Metis and spoke no French. Judge sided with Crown to ensure trial in Regina rather than BC or Ontario as defence asked; this ensured the 6-man, Anglophone, Protestant jury, rather than 12—less chance of hung jury with 6. All lawyers easterners.

B. Riel does seem to have been behaving strangely (explain this) and had spent time in an American asylum. His lawyers thus argued for his insanity—but he was adamant he was sane. Big argument between him and his lawyers meant his defence was not wholehearted or coherent.

C. Riel had formally and legally renounced his loyalty to the Queen and taken on American citizenship years earlier—was 1352 treason law applicable? They could have gone with Canadian treason statutes of 1862 or 1866, but those did not carry death sentence.

IV. Conclusion: Louis Riel was executed, and this is not a surprise in the circumstances.

A. The outcome of the trial was predetermined both by the Canadian federal government's determination to extend full control over the West and by their decision to appease the Anglophone, Protestant population of Ontario. The process was fundamentally flawed in several respects of fairness and legality. The fact that they chose the 1352 statute suggests a desired conclusion.

B. All of the above demonstrates and foreshadows a larger and longer set of struggles, which still continue to the present: federal–provincial, Anglophone–Francophone, and White–First Nation and Metis.

This detailed outline is organized around analytical points, with evidence presented in short narrative accounts.

> **TIP!** All history papers are likely to contain elements both of narrative and analysis.

Draft Outline of a Narrative Essay

It's also possible to organize an essay around a single chronological narrative, in this case an account of the 1885 Northwest Rebellion that focuses on Riel's involvement and includes important analytical points. Here is a simple draft outline of that **narrative essay**:

I. The South Saskatchewan in 1885
    A. General description
    B. The stakeholders and their specific grievances
II. Riel returned from the USA
    A. How and why he came back
    B. Riel's actions as leader
III. The events of the rebellion
    A. Duck Lake, Fish Creek, Batoche
    B. The rebellion ends
IV. The aftermath
    A. Trials, imprisonment, and executions
    B. The effects of rebellion

Complete Narrative Outline

A complete outline of a narrative essay on the rebellion and Riel would include brief references to analytical issues:

I. The South Saskatchewan:
    A. The area was rural, old HBC trading territory; had been buffalo country, but buffalo now disappearing. This

threatened especially the livelihoods of the Metis. Poor harvests in the early 1880s threatened everybody. The territory in the charge of the federal government now, but the government generally not following through on its responsibilities.

B. Short discussion of Saskatchewan society, including Metis, First Nations and White settlers. Discussion of their various grievances, including government reluctance to guarantee Metis title to their own lands and farms, attempts to force First Nations onto reserves, failure to grant much in the way of local government powers, decision to move planned CPR line farther south. The federal government's actions and inactions were largely responsible for the rebellion (an analytical point).

II. Riel returned.

A. He was invited back in 1884 by a delegation of Metis. (Note that these represented a small group of the most militant; most Metis would not be involved in the rebellion.) He was well-educated locally and in Quebec, multi-lingual, and charismatic. Metis himself, his leadership of the resistance to the federal government in 1869–70 had led to the creation of Manitoba as a province, so he was a natural choice even though he'd been in the USA for years (an analytical point).

B. Riel helped in fall of 1884 to create a petition to the federal government—no result. Also instrumental in creating Metis "Bill of Revolutionary Rights" in spring 1885. Comment on the contents of this declaration (analytical point) and on his efforts to get peaceful resolution of the Metis grievances. March 1885, the Metis created provisional government with Riel as president. Analysis of this group and of their immediate actions re: Batoche and HBC Fort Carlton demonstrate increasing militancy.

III. The events of the rebellion.

A. Describe briefly and discuss the military events. Duck Lake (26 March), negotiations with North West

Mounted Police floundered and shots were fired. Dead and wounded on both sides, but police essentially lost. Riel saved them from pursuit. Feds sent in troops and militia, using CPR line—eventually about 5000 of them. First Nations now gearing up for real war. Fish Creek (24 April), FN won—again no pursuit. Batoche (9–12 May), hard fought, but Metis lost.

B. Riel surrendered 15 May—analyze why he didn't just flee to USA. Some First Nations kept going, but big defeat in late May led to surrenders; final surrenders in early July.

IV. The aftermath.

A. Discuss briefly the charges against and trials of the various participants, and speculate on why the Crown used different charges, and even different treason statutes, against them. Concentrate on trial of Riel and of the First Nations' leaders. Briefly outline the sentences.

B. Comment on the effects of the rebellion, which were felt by all parties in the Northwest, but also resonated hugely in Ontario and Quebec. Discuss the results also in Ottawa. End with mention of Riel and the Northwest Rebellion now, and the way in which all of this has helped to shape Canada.

This detailed outline shows how a straightforward chronological narrative can incorporate important analytical content.

REVIEW

1. Create an outline for either an analytical or a narrative paper.
2. If in doubt, create a second outline, from a different angle. Then see which one works best.
3. Structure your paper to suit your purpose and evidence.

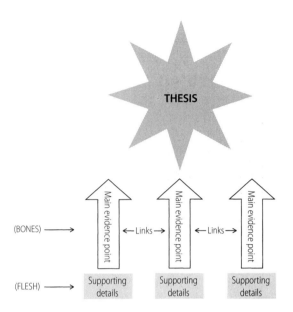

Reporting Faithfully

In the first century BCE, the Roman statesman Cicero laid down two laws for the historian:

> The first . . . is that he shall never dare utter an untruth. The second is that he shall suppress nothing that is true.[35]

These laws remain in force. But good historians also ask questions, and one question comes immediately to mind: how do historians know what is true in any given case? There is no easy answer. Inevitably, some evidence disappears, different sources often contradict one another, and the "truth" can quite legitimately depend on the point of view of the reporter. For example, the missionaries who introduced Christianity to Aboriginal societies may have sincerely believed that they were giving them an incomparable gift. Those societies, however, may have experienced that "gift" as something quite different.

Thus the best we can do is to ensure that we follow a few basic rules in our own work to arrive at an answer that fully reflects the available evidence. Like the law, the rules for faithful representation of the past are subject to variation and interpretation over time, and historical writers do not take a Hippocratic oath to uphold any particular body of rules. Nevertheless, there is a broad general consensus about what is right and what is wrong.

Report Sources Carefully

All scholars build on the work of others. Therefore it is essential to be able to trust that other historians have been faithful to their sources. Above all, it is important to report accurately on the people and events of the past. Both careless reading and sloppy note-taking can lead you to misrepresent history, and readers may accuse you of dishonesty even if the misrepresentation is inadvertent. One way to avoid misunderstanding is to follow these rules:

Make sure that every note you take includes a citation. Every time you jot down a note, write the bibliographic reference next to it. Include as much of the following information as is applicable: full name of author, complete title (including subtitle), series title, edition and volume number, place of publication, publisher, year of publication, and page number. In the case of articles, include the total pages of the article as well as the specific pages to which your notes refer. Whatever medium you use—paper, index cards, or computer—every piece of information should be accompanied by the relevant source reference. Even if you're pressed for time, don't cut corners in your notes; instead, figure out a way to be more efficient. For instance, you could set up a system of abbreviations, or collect all notes from each source together under one bibliographical entry, with a page number for each item, or use colour coding.

> **TIP!** If you use any diagrams, maps, or photographs from other sources, they must also be referenced.

Distinguish clearly between your own words and those of someone else. Always put direct quotations in quotation marks. When you paraphrase (reword) or summarize someone else's material, make sure that you will recognize your own words, and also make sure that your notes and the final assignment are clear that this is a paraphrase or summary, not a record of your own observations.

Copy and paste with care. Before the age of the personal computer, writing and revising a paper was in some ways a more demanding task than it is today. Even so, word-processing technology does present some new organizational challenges. Be especially careful, when copying text from an online source, that you don't accidentally paste it into your draft paper rather than your notes: if you do, you'll run the risk of confusing someone else's words with your own. Always keep your notes in a separate file—and be sure to record the source of any research material that you find online.

Writing technology has changed, but the prohibition on **plagiarism** has not.[36] Since your professor may ask to see your notes and drafts, it's a good idea to print out hard copies of in-progress work as you go along (or at least to save each successive draft under a different file name). Your professor will expect to see the full development of your paper, from your earliest ideas to your latest drafts. Be sure to keep all your notes, no matter how fragmentary some of them may be, and your drafts until the paper has been graded and returned to you.

Treat Others' Ideas with Care and Respect

Researching and writing papers means engaging with the ideas of fellow scholars. As a student you will spend much, if not all, of your time interpreting subjects that many others have interpreted before you. Even if you are the first person to write a history of something, in order to show its full significance, you will have to place your own ideas in the context of a broader historical literature.

Writing is hard work. Therefore it is important to acknowledge the work of others in a respectful way. Historians have conventions for quoting, summarizing, and paraphrasing the works of other scholars. If you follow these conventions carefully, you won't have to go back and check your sources again while you are writing.

Paraphrases and Summaries

Technically speaking, a **paraphrase** uses roughly the same number of words as the original passage, whereas a **summary** uses fewer. Paraphrase is useful when you want to discuss an idea from someone else's work but think that you can say the same thing more clearly.

It can be particularly helpful when you need to translate an archaic or complex quotation. In *The Reluctant Land*, Cole Harris uses both quotation and paraphrase to introduce a concept from the German philosopher Jürgen Habermas:

> In premodern societies, he [Habermas] maintains, people lived "within the horizons of their lifeworld" and could not reach beyond its preinterpreted understandings. In other words, they could interpret and communicate the world only within their own terms of reference.[37]

Summaries are more common than paraphrases in historical writing. They are particularly useful in works of synthesis, where the historian considers the work of others and needs to present their ideas in concise form. In a collection of articles entitled *The Conquest of Acadia, 1710*, Maurice Basque briefly summarizes the work of John Bartlet Brebner (1895–1957), the historian who coined the term "North Atlantic Triangle":

> Generations of historians have been influenced by John Bartlet Brebner's reading of Acadians' reaction to military and political events, specifically that Acadian society was not politically minded.

Basque then summarizes some of Brebner's evidence and discusses his influence on the work of other historians. He also provides citations for further exploration.[38] Summaries can also be useful when the original material is problematic in some way (for instance, if the language is archaic or overly technical). Both summaries and paraphrases indicate to the reader that you have grasped someone else's idea so well that you are able to convey it in your own words. In either case, be sure to include all the relevant points made in the original passage, and also make sure to show that this is indeed a summary or paraphrase, not a presentation of your own ideas or words.

TIP! Using sources clearly and effectively strengthens your argument by showing what you read and how you used the information.

Direct Quotations

Historians usually demonstrate their familiarity with sources by summarizing and paraphrasing, but sometimes they find that a direct quotation is the best way to make a point. Use a direct quotation when correct interpretation depends on the exact wording of the source, or when the original is so effective—so vivid or forceful—that a paraphrase or summary could not do it justice. Otherwise, try to limit your use of quotations. After all, it's your own ideas that the reader wants to find out about.

There are two ways of incorporating quotations. In the first approach, typically, a short quotation will be run into the main text as part of a sentence that identifies the source. Thus if you were writing about the history of gay rights in Canada, you might quote Pierre Trudeau:

> In 1967, Trudeau remarked that "there's no place for the state in the bedrooms of the nation."

Notice that in this example, the quotation is not separated from the body of the sentence by either a comma or a colon. Punctuation should be used only when the grammatical structure of the sentence requires it:

> As Trudeau remarked in 1967, "there's no place for the state in the bedrooms of the nation."

The second approach is normally reserved for passages of more than three lines. A **block quotation** is set off from the main text in a separate block indented 10 spaces from the left margin, with a line space above and below. The sentence before the quotation should introduce it, and the sentence after it should link the quotation to the text that follows. For example, in *Lethal Legacy: Current Native Controversies in Canada*, J.R. Miller quotes from the section of the Royal Proclamation of 1763 that was designed to prevent unscrupulous buyers from cheating Aboriginal peoples out of their lands:

Too often Thirteen Colonies purchasers could brandish their "deed" and insist that the state help to enforce their spurious title against indigenous resistance. The Royal Proclamation aimed to prevent such outrages by decreeing that private citizens could not obtain Native land.

> And whereas Great Frauds and Abuses have been committed in purchasing Land of the Indians, to the great Prejudice of our Interests, and to the great Dissatisfaction of the said Indians; In order, therefore, to prevent such Irregularities for the future, and to the End that the Indians may be convinced of our Justice and determined Resolution to remove all reasonable Cause of Discontent, We do, with the Advice of our Privy Council strictly enjoin and require, that no private Person do presume to make any Purchase from the said Indians of any Lands reserved to the said Indians. . . .

Only the Crown could legally get land from Aboriginal people. And, even then, the Crown's representative had to do so in a public way. Said the Proclamation, if "any of the said Indians should be inclined to dispose of the said Lands, the same shall be Purchased only for Us in our Name, at some public Meeting or Assembly of the said Indians, to be held for the Purpose by the Governor or Commander in Chief of our Colony."[39]

In this case of a longer quotation, the paragraphs that precede and follow the indented quotation seamlessly integrate it into Miller's text. Notice that Miller carefully places his quotation into context first and then summarizes its meaning and significance.

Be Fair to Your Sources

Historians often need to abridge the passages they quote in order to make them fit into their own material. To indicate omissions they use ellipsis points, which look like three periods (. . .). One basic rule governs the use of **ellipses**: any abridged quotation must be faithful to the original, full quotation.

TIP! If your abridged quotation comes at the end of your sentence, then when you add your period you will have four dots instead of three. (See the Miller quotation above.) Similarly, if your abridged sentence includes pieces from more than one sentence of the original text, then also use the four dots in any spot where you omitted both words and period. (See the Mackenzie quotation below.)

This is not as easy as it sounds. Suppose you are writing a five-page essay on the 1837 rebellion in Upper Canada and have decided to focus on the reformers' complaints concerning Britain's treatment of the colony. In a newspaper article most likely written by William Lyon Mackenzie they enumerated a long list of grievances, which included the following:

- The King of England has forbidden his governors to pass laws of immediate and pressing importance, unless suspended in their operation till his assent should be obtained; and when so suspended, he has utterly neglected to attend to them. He has interfered with the freedom of elections, and appointed elections to be held at places dangerous, unconvenient and unsafe for the people to assemble at, for the purpose of fatiguing them into his measures, through the agency of pretended representatives; and has through his legislative council, prevented provision from being made for quiet and peaceable elections, as in the case of the late returns at Beverley.
- He has dissolved the late House of Assembly for opposing with manly firmness Sir Francis Head's invasion of the right of the people to a wholesome control over the revenue, and for insisting that the persons conducting the government should be responsible for their official conduct to the country through its representatives.
- He has endeavoured to prevent the peopling of this province and its advancement in wealth; for that purpose obstructing the laws for the naturalization of foreigners, refusing to pass others to encourage their migration hither, and raising the

conditions of new appropriations of the public lands, large tracts of which he has bestowed upon unworthy persons his favourites, while deserving settlers from Germany and other countries have been used cruelly.

- He has rendered the administration of Justice liable to suspicion and distrust, by obstructing laws for establishing a fair trial by Jury, by refusing to exclude the chief criminal judge from interfering in political business, and by selecting as the judiciary violent and notorious partisans of his arbitrary power.[40]

Mackenzie's language is so rich that you would like to quote the entire document, but that would take up too much of your limited space. Therefore you decide to abridge his text, using ellipses to indicate omissions:

> Enumerating their complaints in a newspaper article (most likely written by Mackenzie), the reformers charged that "The King of England has forbidden his governors to pass laws of immediate and pressing importance, unless suspended in their operation till his assent should be obtained. . . . He has interfered with the freedom of elections. . . . He has dissolved the late House of Assembly. . . . He has endeavoured to prevent the peopling of this province and its advancement in wealth. . . . He has rendered the administration of Justice liable to suspicion and distrust. . . ."

But notice that your sentence does not flow well into the quotation: there is a jarring difference between your verb tense and Mackenzie's. You could eliminate the problem by removing the word "has," except that then you'd be stuck with the incorrect form of the verb "to forbid." In addition, writing "The King of England" and then having the quotation repeat "he" as the subject sounds awkward and unnatural. You could solve these problems by inserting some square-bracketed words of your own so that your sentence flows naturally into the quotation from Mackenzie. The brackets tell readers that these are not Mackenzie's exact words, but that they still convey Mackenzie's exact meaning:

In a newspaper article that was most likely written by Mackenzie, the reformers listed a number of complaints about Britain's treatment of Upper Canada. They charged that "The King . . . [had] forbidden his governors to pass laws of immediate and pressing importance, unless suspended in their operation till his assent should be obtained . . . interfered with the freedom of elections . . . dissolved the late House of Assembly . . . endeavoured to prevent the peopling of . . . [the] province and its advancement in wealth . . . [and] rendered the administration of justice liable to suspicion and distrust. . . ."

This quotation is faithful to Mackenzie's exact meaning, even though it abridges his text with ellipses and brackets. Not every abridgement is so faithful, however. It would have been unfaithful to use ellipses in the following manner: "The King of England has forbidden his governors to pass laws of immediate and pressing importance . . . for the purpose of fatiguing [the people] into his measures." This version would be unfair to Mackenzie, because the first portion of the original quotation actually introduced an entirely different set of ideas: "unless suspended in their operation till his assent should be obtained; and when so suspended, he has utterly neglected to attend to them."

In the same way, it would have been unfaithful to write only that "The King of England has forbidden his governors to pass [necessary] laws . . ." because you would be altering the sense of the original text: "[He] has forbidden his governors to pass laws of immediate and pressing importance . . ." If you need to be so concise, summarizing Mackenzie in your own words would be preferable to inserting different words directly into his original writing.

Using Quotation Marks

Quotation marks seem to cause more confusion than any other form of punctuation (with the possible exception of apostrophes). When you run a quotation into your text, place the words inside double quotation marks:

Borden called Canada "a nation that is not a nation."

For a quotation within a quotation, use single quotation marks to delineate the parts. Note that as in the following example this may mean that you have a single quotation mark and a double quotation mark together:

> In her account of the post–First World War Paris Peace Conference, *Paris 1919: Six Months That Changed the World*, Margaret MacMillan writes that Canadian Prime Minister Borden saw "Canada as 'a nation that is not a nation,'" a situation he hoped "'to alter.'"[41]

The placement of other punctuation in relation to the quotation marks varies. Periods and commas should be placed *inside* the quotation marks. However, question marks and exclamation points should be placed *outside* unless they were part of the original quotation. Colons and semicolons also go outside the quotation marks.

Be Careful Not to Plagiarize

Unfaithful quotation is a serious problem, but the harshest condemnation is reserved for plagiarists. In the ancient Mediterranean world, *plagiarii* were pirates whose crimes included the kidnapping of young children.[42] When plagiarists claim someone else's ideas as their own, they steal someone else's brainchild. Historians do not tolerate this behaviour. In their efforts to combat plagiarism, some universities require that students submit their papers to text-matching software, and most enforce severe disciplinary policies. At the very least, the plagiarist will fail the assignment in question, but the penalties can include expulsion from the university and a record of the offence on the student's permanent academic record.

Plagiarism is infrequent among professional scholars, who share a commitment to honesty across all the disciplines. Even so, it does occur from time to time.

Direct plagiarism. Direct plagiarism occurs when one writer takes another writer's exact words and passes them off as his or her own. Direct plagiarism is often easy for an informed reader to spot.

Indirect plagiarism. Indirect plagiarism is more difficult to recognize. It occurs most often when writers paraphrase someone else's work too closely. In such cases the plagiarist inserts an occasional new word or phrase to make the writing slightly different, but retains the original structure of the sentence or paragraph. For example, here is an original passage taken from Colin M. Coates's article "Commemorating the Woman Warrior of New France, Madeleine de Verchères, 1696–1930." Discussing a monument to de Verchères, Coates writes:

> Gazing upon the statue . . . , no one would mistake her for a man: the swirling dress, the feminine facial features, the long braids dangling down her back, the pubescent breasts, all precluded misinterpretation. Only her (men's) hat and massive gun hinted otherwise.[43]

The following overly close paraphrase would amount to indirect plagiarism:

> Looking at the memorial, no observer could take her for a male. Her womanly clothes and appearance would prevent any mistake. Nothing but her hat and gun suggested masculinity.

This would be indirect plagiarism even if it were accompanied by a citation acknowledging Coates's work, because the writer does not clearly indicate how much has been borrowed from it. Here is an example of an acceptable paraphrase:

> Colin Coates remarks that this is clearly a statue of a woman, arguing that the clothes and personal appearance, in fact everything except the "hat and massive gun," make it impossible to think otherwise.

TIP! Be very careful—indirect plagiarism often happens by accident.

With the appropriate citation, the explicit reference to Coates makes the source of the sentence perfectly clear.

Inadvertent plagiarism. What if you accidentally neglect to put quotation marks around a passage from someone else's writing? What if you forget to provide a citation when you summarize someone else's writing? Think for a minute about your readers. All they see are the words in front of them. They don't see you frantically trying to finish your paper at two in the morning. By the time you apologize for the oversight, it will be too late. When readers detect a mistake, they will instinctively form the worst possible impression of you. Remember, it is entirely your own responsibility to avoid plagiarism, not theirs to guess at your intentions.

In 2002, two prominent historians, Stephen Ambrose and Doris Kearns Goodwin, were accused of plagiarism. Both defended themselves by admitting to sloppy research practices. This is a believable defence, but it is also deeply embarrassing, and the careers of both authors were damaged. The "sloppiness" defence highlights the relationship between plagiarism and lack of discipline.

Try to avoid situations that may be conducive to plagiarism. Make sure from the very beginning of your research process to include full citations for every work on which you are taking notes. Don't wait until the last minute to research and write history assignments. Make sure that you have plenty of time to document your sources correctly and double-check them to make sure, even when you are certain that everything is in order. You may be surprised at how often you will find little mistakes.

It's your responsibility to use your sources honestly and fairly, and "I didn't mean to" is no excuse. To make matters worse, it will be much easier for readers to prove your guilt than for you to prove your innocence.

Academic dishonesty. Obviously, you should never submit anything with your name on it that was written in whole or in part by somebody else. This includes any paper bought from an essay writing service, downloaded from the Internet, borrowed from a friend or found in a fraternity file. If you pass off someone else's work as your own, you are a plagiarist. According to most university regulations, anyone who supplies you with such a paper is a plagiarist as well.

There are other acts of academic dishonesty that closely resemble plagiarism. Occasionally it may be possible to submit the same paper in two courses, but only if you have obtained permission in advance from both instructors: otherwise you will be writing one paper while secretly attempting to get credit for two. In addition, an instructor's permission is usually required if you want to submit a paper written in collaboration with another student. If you are allowed to work with another student, you must never try pass off the other student's writing as your own.

Don't Give Unnecessary Citations

After reading the preceding section, are you now so frightened that you feel you have to include a source citation in every sentence you write? If so, remember that the purpose of the essay is to set out your ideas. The main argument is expected to be yours and should need few or no notes.

Don't go overboard with citations. Provide them always when you cite statistics or obscure facts, when you quote directly, paraphrase, or summarize someone else's work, or when you are consciously borrowing the structure or point of view of someone else's approach to a topic. There is no need to provide a citation for a fact that is common knowledge: for example, that the Allies landed at Normandy on 6 June 1944, or that the CPR played a crucial part in the settlement of western Canada. If what you thought was common knowledge ("Columbus first sailed across the Atlantic in 1492") turns out to be a bit more doubtful than you expected, though, a citation is a good idea.

There is also no need to provide a citation for more specialized knowledge that is familiar to anyone working "within the field." For example, most people probably do not know the dates and dynasties of the Roman emperors, but this is common knowledge to historians of the Roman world, and not particularly open to interpretation or disagreement. Of course, if you are unsure whether something is common knowledge, there's no harm in playing it safe and providing a citation.[44]

Choose a Citation System that Suits Your Readers

There are only two rules that apply to all source citations: the format you choose must make it easy for readers to check your sources, and you must use it consistently. Otherwise the rules vary widely, partly because many publishers have their own "house styles" and partly because individual institutions, departments, and even instructors often have their own preferred style guides. If your professor has not specified a **citation system**, be sure to ask what is expected.

Students are sometimes confused to find that that their history instructor will not accept the citation system they have been taught in other courses. For example, the standard approach in sociology is to place the author's name, date of publication, and page number in parentheses after a quotation, summary, or paraphrase. In many social sciences, the title of the work is also included. Although this system can work well in some cases, most historians use sequential footnotes or **endnotes**, following the guidelines laid out by Kate L. Turabian in *A Manual for Writers of Research Papers, Theses, and Dissertations*, 8th ed. (Chicago: University of Chicago Press, 2013). A brief version of it is available at www.press.uchicago.edu/books/turabian/turabian_citation guide.html. "Turabian," as it is usually called, is a concise version of the rules set out in *The Chicago Manual of Style*, which is widely considered the authoritative guide for preparing manuscripts.[45] Both books can be found in any academic library, and will be stocked in most university and college bookshops.

The reason historians tend to prefer the notes and bibliography system is that their source references are often too long and complex to fit neatly into a parenthetical citation. Not only are sources such as letters and diaries difficult to cite concisely, but historians frequently refer to more than one source at a time. To include so much information in the text would be distracting and annoying for readers. Thus most history instructors prefer that students use either footnotes or endnotes, both of which are easy to create using a word-processing program. For some of the most commonly used citations, see Appendix B. If the source you are working with does not fit any of the models outlined in the appendix, refer to either Turabian or *The Chicago Manual*, both of which offer much more comprehensive listings. They also cover the in-text author–date citation systems that are more commonly used in literature and the social sciences, notably the Modern Language Association (MLA) style and the American Psychological Association (APA) style. Note that the recent seventh edition of the *MLA Handbook* includes a section on endnotes and footnotes. Earlier editions cover this information in an appendix.

To show some "real-life" referencing, here is an excerpt from a recent undergraduate paper on the history of the Britannia Beach mines in British Columbia, by Justin Elsworth:

TIP! Notice in this example the tiny **superscript** note numbers, each of which corresponds to its numbered footnote or endnote.

While the natives used "copper for decorations [such as] ear spools, beads, and . . . sheets of copper used in potlatches,"[1] some native legends say Britannia was never fished or hunted at because it was cursed.[2] Such a curse holds true for one of the first discoverers of Britannia, a fur trapper named Oliver Furry, who had been drawn to the area by the BC Gold Rush. Furry made claims in the Jane Basin area with a man named Joseph Boscowitz in 1898, but returned in 1901 to find that 7/10ths interest in the Boscowitz holdings had been sold for $35,000 to Howard Walters of Montana.[3] Engaged in legal disputes over Britannia, Furry became increasingly violent because of stress over the claim of ownership and was ultimately institutionalized in New Westminster.[4] In a cruel twist of fate, the courts ruled that Furry had "held a fifty percent interest"[5] in 1906, but unfortunately Furry had died the previous year in the asylum. Furry, like so many others during the BC Gold Rush era, would never prosper from his finds.

Here are the footnote or endnote references for this excerpt:
1. Florida Ann Town, *The Lively Ghost of Howe Sound* (Port Coquitlam, BC: Bookus Press, 2000), 4.
2. *Britannia: A Company Town*, VHS, directed by David Vaisbord (Montreal: National Film Board of Canada, 2000).
3. Town, *Lively Ghost*, 23.
4. Doreen Armitage, *Around the Howe Sound: A History of Howe Sound-Whistler* (Madeira Park, BC: Harbour Publishing, 1997), 102.

5. Bruce Ramsey, *Britannia: The Story of a Mine*, 2nd. ed. (Victoria: Britannia Beach Historical Society, 2004), 26.

> **TIP!** As notes 1 and 3 demonstrate, the first note entry for each work gives complete publishing information. Any subsequent reference to the same work can be shortened.

Here are the bibliography entries for the same sources:

Armitage, Doreen. *Around the Howe Sound: A History of Howe Sound-Whistler*. Madeira Park, BC: Harbour Publishing, 1997.

Britannia: A Company Town. Directed by David Vaisbord. Montreal: National Film Board of Canada, 2000. Videocassette.

Ramsey, Bruce. *Britannia: The Story of a Mine*. Victoria: Britannia Beach Historical Society, 2004.

Town, Florida Ann. *The Lively Ghost of Howe Sound*. Port Coquitlam, BC: Bookus Press, 2000.

REVIEW

1. Record and report your sources with care.
2. When you paraphrase or summarize someone else's argument, make it clear.
3. Use the appropriate citation system.
4. Don't forget the bibliography.

Build an Argument

A historical essay needs to do more than state a thesis and present evidence to support it. A good historical essay will lead its readers through its argument so persuasively that they will be convinced of the truth of your conclusion. This is true too for all historical assignments: you should always show your point of view, develop your argument. An argument is not a dispute or disagreement: it is an idea that is developed over the course of an assignment. An argument must capture and hold the reader's attention.

Start to Write a First Draft

The complete outlines in Chapter 4 are the frameworks for two sustained arguments. A good outline will show how each section of the essay is related to the main argument. As you are thinking about the overall outline of your essay, check your sources for evidence supporting your thesis, and compose paragraphs around those points. You don't have to start with the introduction; in fact, you may well write it last. As you grapple with your sources, you will discover new things about them, things that may make your first version of the introduction obsolete by the time you finish the body of the text.

While you are writing the first draft, adding analysis and information, stand back occasionally and think about how your argument is evolving. Is it developing in a reasonable way? If not—if you find that you have modified your line of argument in some way—don't worry. Just go back to the beginning, adjust your thesis statement if necessary, and then check the entire argument for consistency.

Grab Your Reader's Attention, but Do It Gently

Every reader asks, "Why should I read this?" "Why should I care?" Writers must give their readers reasons to care. Many historians use the beginning of an essay or book to connect their scholarly interests to broader academic and political debates. For example, in a 1997 article called "Taming Aboriginal Sexuality: Gender, Power and Race in British Columbia, 1850–1900," Jean Barman begins with a courtroom scene and frames it in a way that is bound to grab the reader's attention:

> In July 1996 I listened in a Vancouver court room as Catholic Bishop Hubert O'Conner defended himself against charges of having raped or indecently assaulted four young Aboriginal women three decades earlier. His assertion of ignorance when asked what one of the complainants had been wearing on the grounds that "as you know, I'm a celibate man" encapsulated his certainty that he had done nothing wrong. He admitted to sexual relations with two of the women, but the inference was clear: they had made him do it. They had dragged him down and led him astray. The temptation exercised by their sexuality was too great for any mere man, even a priest and residential school principal, to resist.
>
> I returned home from that day, and subsequent days in the court room, deeply troubled. I might have been reading any of hundreds of similar accounts written over the past century and more about Aboriginal women in British Columbia. This essay represents my first attempt to come to terms with Bishop O'Conner and his predecessors. . . . My interest is not in Bishop O'Conner's guilt or innocence in a court of law, but, rather, in tracing the lineage of his attitudes in the history of British Columbia.[46]

Notice Barman's tone. She addresses topics of universal interest like sex and racism, and specific incidents that could cause revulsion, but she does so calmly and methodically. You don't need to drop a bomb to get your reader's attention, and you don't need to be emotional or sensationalist. Be relevant, but be gentle. Readers prefer writing that they find balanced, trustworthy, and authoritative. If you suspect that they may disagree with you, it's your job to bring them around. Put them in the right frame of mind to listen to your argument.

State Your Intellectual Interests Early

> **TIP!** Write about what interests you, and be clear why it should interest your readers.

In the example above, Barman first catches the reader's attention by frankly stating the disturbing facts of the case. She then quickly shifts the focus and begins to outline her intellectual interest in it. Your readers will also expect you to give them a sense of your intellectual interests. What are the broader historical problems that your essay addresses? Why have you chosen your specific topic to explore those interests? What argument will you be developing over the course of your essay? If you don't address these questions at the beginning of your essay, you will run the risk of losing your readers.

One introduction that answers these questions comes from a book by Ken Coates, P. Whitney Lackenbauer, William R. Morrison, and Greg Poelzer entitled *Arctic Front: Defending Canada in the Far North*. After a brief introduction in which the authors express their collective frustration over the lack of a clear understanding of Canada's role in the Arctic north despite debate on the subject recurring over more than a century, they go on to outline the origins of "the contemporary debate" and why it is important for Canada and for the world:[47]

> The High Arctic may well be the last true empty space on the planet.... where tiny islands, the shape of the continental shelf, and longitudinal projections have suddenly become the stuff of international politics. There may be a lot at stake, if there truly are large deposits of oil and gas in the North. On the other hand, it may turn out to be, as in the past, much ado about a lot of ice and cold water. The Russians, though, are deadly serious—and the

West continues to misunderstand and underestimate both that nation and its leadership. The Americans are intractably stubborn on both military issues and questions of international straits, and—if we believe journalists and academics—the pesky Danes and others (including the Russians and Chinese) cast covetous looks at Canadian areas of interest.... [T]his is not simply a replay of nineteenth- or twentieth-century contests. There is much more at play—oil, gas, northern passageways, and a painful illustration of how ill-prepared we are for Arctic disputes in the twenty-first. The issues are global, in the form of the climate change debate; local, through indigenous claims and self-government initiatives; and circumpolar, in terms of military issues and competition for northern resources.[48]

The authors start by emphasizing the unusual situation of the North, which they present as technologically undeveloped but potentially of massive economic value. This should catch the attention of anyone who is interested in Canada's economic health. They mention (and later in the book will follow in detail) the historical debates over northern sovereignty. Anyone who has wondered about the relevance of history to modern-day diplomatic, political, and economic issues should be interested in reading this book. Finally, and still in the introduction, Coates et al., connect the past not only to the present but to the future, reinforcing the economic and military urgency of clarifying and claiming Canada's northern sovereignty.

Implicitly, while arguing that Canada needs to change its tactics and defend its claims to the North far more vigorously, Coates, Lackenbauer, Morrison, and Poelzer argue that historical perspectives inform the modern debate on the role of the West in Canada. They are not trying to attack anyone, but rather to drive home the necessity, for policy-makers, of historical knowledge. They start to build their case very quickly by telling their audience why they should be interested, how future prosperity and national security might be affected by past decisions and present policies, and why it is in Canada's interest to address its claims to sovereignty in the High Arctic.

Build Your Essay with Good Paragraphs

A paragraph is much more than an indented block of text. It should contribute to the overall argument of the essay by presenting evidence and developing inferences based on it. The best paragraphs have three components:

A transition from the preceding paragraph. Readers want to know why they are moving from one paragraph to the next. Good paragraphs are connected to each other with one or two **transition sentences**: signposts that remind readers where they have been and point to where they are going. Here is an example of an effective transition from student Alice Gorton's recent lower-division paper on prostitution and consumerism in Victorian Britain:

> Prostitutes were exploited on the grounds of being essential goods needed to facilitate male sexuality. Their role caused a widespread debate in Victorian Britain, one that could not have been possible without the relative increase of education and wealth.
>
> The emerging consumerist ideology and view of female sexuality as a commodity came to a head with the Contagious Disease Acts and the legalization of prostitution in 1864.

In this example of transition, Gorton ends a discussion of increasing education and wealth in Victorian Britain and links the economic point to the next topic, the introduction of the Infectious Disease Acts.[49]

TIP! Think historically—don't impose your twenty-first-century sense of morality or justice on people from other cultures and past times. Try to understand and explain them rather than standing in judgment over them.

A statement of the paragraph's point. Each paragraph presents and develops a point that supports the overall argument of the essay. In the paper quoted above, Gorton introduced one paragraph with a topic sentence clearly delineating the major point that she would discuss: "Increased prostitution rates in Victorian Britain can be attributed to industrial expansion and urbanization."

Supporting evidence. What sort of evidence do you have to support your argument? Present the information from your sources that has allowed you to make historical inferences.

> **TIP!** Think of yourself as the leader, drawing your readers along the path of your argument. Make sure you give them the evidence they need to follow you through your argument and arrive at the same destination—your conclusion.

Gorton goes on from her topic sentence above to discuss the effects of developing industrialization, which drew large numbers of people into the growing cities of England in search of work, the alienating nature of cities for those without family or other support networks, the vulnerability of women and girls in low-income occupations and their difficult social place as they were unable to conform to the "socially and politically sanctioned" nineteenth-century domestic ideal for women.

Of course there is no formula for combining these components. Sometimes the argument will be located in a transition sentence, and sometimes it will appear in its own thesis sentence. Sometimes it will be presented before the evidence and sometimes after. The best historical writers blend transition, argument, and evidence so seamlessly that they carry the reader with them, progressively building their case as they move from one paragraph to the next.

Define Your Key Terms Early

Never assume that your audience will understand important terms to mean the same thing that you do. Define your central concepts as soon as you introduce them, preferably at the beginning of your essay.

You may find that you can use a definition as a springboard to discuss the complexities of your subject.

Defining uncommon terms. Sometimes you will need to define specialized or foreign terms that your audience might not recognize. In a 2001 article called "Plunder or Harmony? On Merging European and Native Views of Early Contact," Toby Morantz discusses a common First Nations' distinction between *atiukan* and *tipachiman* accounts of their own history. Knowing that most of her readers will not be familiar with these words, Morantz explains that while the *atiukan* part of the oral tradition "refers to myths, stories concerning the creation of the world when people and animals were not differentiated," the *tipachiman* accounts "are about real people—living, or their ancestors— but not necessarily without reference to what Western thinking would label the supernatural."[50] Morantz's definition is clear, but she also implicitly suggests that the First Nations' perspectives of reality are not exactly the same as those from European backgrounds. Thus Morantz uses her definition to invite her readers to consider the larger issue of competing views and interpretations of reality, which is a central part of her argument.

> **TIP!** Note in the Morantz excerpt above that we italicize words from foreign languages. The exception would be words that commonly turn up in English usage, for example "café" or "gesundheit."

Redefining common terms. In addition to defining unfamiliar terms, sometimes you may need to redefine standard English words. This is exactly what William Cronon does in his book *Changes in the Land: Indians, Colonists, and the Ecology of New England. The Canadian Oxford Dictionary* defines "landscape" as "natural or imaginary scenery as seen in a broad view," but Cronon uses the word more broadly. Cronon's New Englanders saw that the "landscape was a visible confirmation of the state of human society."[51] An English landscape, a way of viewing and ordering the world, prevailed over an indigenous American landscape.

Set an Appropriate Tone

All writers must build a relationship with their readers. The best way to establish rapport is to find an appropriate, trustworthy tone.

Avoid the first-person singular. Generally speaking, historians don't write in the first-person singular. They recognize that personal biases enter historical writing—there is usually no need to overemphasize it. Therefore they rarely, if ever, make the personal angle explicit. You should follow their lead. If you have a statement to make—say, "Margaret Ormsby ignored the role of the First Nations in the development of British Columbian society"—don't preface it with "I think that" or "In my opinion." Just go ahead and say it. Readers will have no difficulty inferring that this is your opinion.

In most cases, historians use the first-person singular only when their personal experience is in some way relevant to their subject matter and they need to explain their relationship to it. Jean Barman's first-person approach in the article cited earlier in this chapter is one example of an appropriate use of the first-person singular.

Similarly, Carl Degler begins his book *In Search of Human Nature*, about racial thinking in anthropology, as follows: "Like most white Americans of my sex and class (the son of a fireman) and my generation (born in 1921) I came into a world that soon made me a racist and a sexist."[52] He does this both to focus attention on his subject and to inform readers of his personal investment in it—a factor that they may wish to take into account when they evaluate his arguments.

Be judicious and dispassionate. All historians pass judgment on their subjects, but they usually try not to be too heavy-handed. For example, suppose you are writing about someone who is known to have committed a horrible crime or otherwise behaved poorly. If the evidence speaks for itself, there is no need for you to make your judgment explicit: concentrate on presenting the facts and let readers form their own opinions.

Andrea Geiger is a historian whose book *Subverting Exclusion* studies the experiences of Japanese immigrants to the United States and Canada. Geiger concentrates on the ways in which racial- and caste-based prejudices persistently relegated immigrants of Japanese descent to low status in North America. Thus she discusses in detail the inherited attitudes of the immigrants themselves and also the systemic legal barriers that they faced in North America. As she remarks in her introduction, Asian immigrants in general and Japanese ones in particular faced a more difficult battle with prejudice than most other immigrants to North America. "Anti-Asian prejudice was written into law and integrated into the very fabric of society to a degree that distinguished it from the challenges that others faced."[53] Geiger goes on to examine exactly how prejudices and other preconceptions negatively affected the Asian immigrant experience in nineteenth- and twentieth-century North America. She does not hit her readers over their heads with her opinion that this was wrong—she tells the story and allows her readers to come to their own conclusions.

Sometimes it is enough just to describe a horrible event for your readers to understand that you find it repugnant. Afua Cooper begins her exploration of slavery in eighteenth-century Quebec as follows:

> In April 1734, Montreal burned. A slave woman, Marie-Joseph Angélique, was the main suspect. She was arrested by the police and hauled in front of the court, and she endured a two-month trial. Throughout the trial, however, Angélique maintained her innocence. At the end of the ordeal, she was found guilty and condemned to be tortured, have her right hand cut off, and then be burned alive. Her sentence was appealed in the Conseil Supérieur, the highest court in the land, and the judges of the Conseil modified the grisly sentence—the slave woman was only to be tortured and then hanged.[54]

Cooper does not need to state that the trial and sentence were unjust. She does not overemphasize the vulnerability of the condemned woman or ridicule the Conseil Supérieur's concept of mercy. She makes her argument simply by recounting the facts, trusting that readers will find them as repugnant as she does.

Treat Other Writers with Consideration

Scholarship thrives on lively debate and open disagreement, but it depends on mutual respect and careful consideration. When you write about other historians, give them the same respect that you would if you were speaking to them in person. Never oversimplify, misrepresent, or ridicule another historian's argument, no matter how strongly you may disagree, and never make personal attacks on opponents. You don't have to agree with them, but you must be polite and you must be fair.

> **TIP!** Don't feel that you must agree with professional historians' opinions or interpretations, or even with those of your professor—scholarly debate is the lifeblood of history. You probably won't be 100 per cent "right" either—and that's fine. Be sure that the research backing your opinion is solid, though!

Account for Counter-Arguments

Don't just select one argument and then ignore all other possibilities. When you acknowledge the existence of alternative interpretations you increase the credibility and complexity of your own work. Your readers won't think you are weak; they will think you are fair. In fact, readers may already be aware of possible objections to your argument, or other sources that contradict it, and they will expect you to deal with them.

By the very nature of their work, historians know that no interpretation is flawless. In a short essay, it is often effective to note the main counter-arguments, and explain briefly why your argument remains more convincing. In a longer essay, thesis, or book, authors often address multiple counter-arguments as they consider the evidence.

One example of counter-argumentation can be found in Robert McElvaine's book *Eve's Seed: Biology, the Sexes, and the Course of History*. McElvaine reviews evidence from prehistory and evolutionary psychology suggesting that for most of human history, females

> **TIP!** Again, think of yourself as drawing your readers down a path. Dealing effectively with counter-arguments is like closing off side roads so that your readers will go where you want them to and not get lost or sidetracked.

were not necessarily subordinate to males. He argues that male domination is not natural, but can be explained historically as a by-product of the Agricultural Revolution, starting around 10,000 BCE. According to McElvaine, it was when men lost their roles as hunters that, out of insecurity and envy, they turned to misogyny.

To make this argument, McElvaine has to address two counter-arguments: that human behaviour is completely determined by biology, and the opposite argument, that every individual is born with a clean slate, and that nurture is the determining factor.

McElvaine wants to demonstrate that both nature and nurture are important. First, he engages the two opposing positions with a joke. Quoting his own father in an early chapter title, he writes that people are "90 percent nature and 90 percent nurture." Next he moves to consider the "nurture" position:

> The reason that so many liberals have clung to their insistence that human nature should be ignored is…a fundamental misapprehension concerning the implications of human nature. They have feared that the admission of the existence of innate characteristics will lead to findings on how people *differ*. In fact, the real meaning of human nature, as [Franz] Boas understood, is to be found in showing the ways in which people are *alike*. As Robert Wright has said, unlike the old social Darwinists, "today's Darwinian anthropologists, in scanning the world's peoples, focus less on surface differences among cultures than on deep unities."

Now McElvaine turns to the "conservative" position advocated by "sociobiologists" such as Richard Dawkins and Edward Wilson, who believe that social behaviour is determined by Darwinian natural selection:

Conservatives seize on the principle of natural selection to maintain that everything that exists should be left alone, because it was made that way by the god of adaptation. But this is not so. It ignores genetic drift, whereby characteristics come into being that provide no evolutionary advantage, but also no disadvantage, and so survive despite Darwinian selection, not because of it. The actual essence of the Darwinian principle of selection is not that a trait must be well adapted in order to survive, but that it not be *poorly* adapted relative to other traits. It is possible for some features to continue to develop after they have fulfilled their original evolutionary function. Human intellectual ability is probably an example of this. It grew far beyond what was necessary for human survival in the eons during which it was physically developing (although perhaps not beyond or even up to what is necessary for survival in the nuclear age; indeed it may yet prove to be ultimately maladaptive by destroying the species).

McElvaine's summary of the liberal and conservative positions is balanced and fair-minded, even though he strongly disagrees with both. By reporting accurately and engaging opposing arguments, he makes it more likely that liberals and conservatives alike will be persuaded to consider his argument: that liberal views on social and gender equality are actually supported by biological evidence.[55]

Lead Your Readers to an Interesting Conclusion

Over the course of your essay, all your detailed evidence and analysis should serve to reinforce your main argument. By the time you reach your concluding paragraph, your readers will be ready for you to put your ideas back into a broader context.

There is no formula for a concluding paragraph. Even so, there are certain expectations. First, a conclusion ought to address the "Who cares?" question once again. How are your findings significant? How might they change the way the readers think?

Second, a conclusion should not simply repeat the introduction. If the essay has truly developed its central idea, there should be an interesting new way to sum it up.

One example of an interesting conclusion can be found in Mercedes Steedman's article "The Red Petticoat Brigade," on RCMP surveillance of the Ladies' Auxiliary of the Mine, Mill and Smelter Workers Union of Sudbury, Ontario, in the Cold War era. Why would the RCMP spend decades monitoring an organization devoted as much to bake sales as to labour activism? Steedman concludes that the surveillance reflected contemporary fear of the perceived threats posed by communism, as well as postwar concern over the proper place of women in society:

> **TIP!** Make sure that your conclusion relates clearly to your overall thesis and to the evidence you have presented in your argument.

> The RCMP surveillance of innocuous social groups was part of a larger social construction of Cold War culture, one that turned neighbour against neighbour and generated a general climate of suspicion. In this way RCMP surveillance served to constrain the character of working-class post-war activism for both men and women. For working-class women activists, these constraints of post-war "normalcy" meant that women who openly advocated women's equality and social justice were immediately suspect, even when they were holding tea parties. Yet Mine Mill women did actively promote a greater voice for women of the day. Through the auxiliary movement, working-class women worked for the cessation of weapons testing, for full disarmament, and for the creation of conditions that, as Dorothy McDonald reported, "would enable women to fulfill their roles in society, as mothers, workers, and citizens which includes the right to work, the protection of motherhood, equal rights with regards to marriage, children and property."[56]

Steedman summarizes her argument and then goes beyond it to suggest that the Mine Mill women were in fact early activists in what would later become known as the women's liberation movement.

REVIEW

1. Be prepared to write several drafts.
2. Explain your purpose clearly.
3. Structure your argument carefully.
4. Define your terms.
5. Deal with counter-arguments.
6. Make your conclusion count.

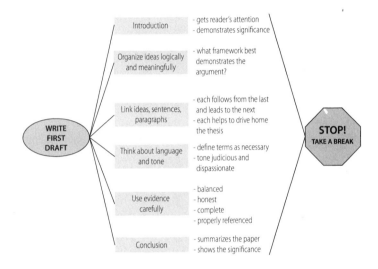

Narrative Techniques

You may decide to organize your essay either as one long narrative or as a series of short narratives illustrating particular points of analysis. Narrative structure is important in either case.

Tell a Story

Every narrative has some easily recognized features: a narrator, one or more characters, a setting, and a plot that unfolds chronologically, over time. Historical narratives share these features with other forms of storytelling, including novels and epic poems.

One of the first historical narratives was written in the fifth century BCE by a Greek adventurer and storyteller named Herodotus. He used dramatic tension and colourful description to help his readers imagine the past. When he came to recount how the emperor Xerxes and his army destroyed the small contingent of Spartans guarding the pass at Thermopylae, he did not simply say that the outnumbered Spartans were brave and fought to the death. Instead he told how the Spartans responded when the massive Persian forces came into sight, not fleeing but calmly continuing to comb their long hair in preparation for battle. He also reported an anecdote told of a Spartan soldier named Dieneces:

> TIP! Think! What do you want your reader to know? Why? What will be the best way to tell your story?

It is said before the battle he was told by a native of Trachis that, when the Persians shot their arrows, there were so many of them that they hid the sun. Dieneces, however, quite unmoved by the thought of the strength of the Persian army, merely remarked: "This is pleasant news . . . if the Persians hide the sun, we shall have our battle in the shade."[57]

Write a Narrative to Support an Argument

Herodotus was not merely telling a story about a particular battle. He was selecting anecdotes and stories in order to build an argument for a particular interpretation of the event. The best storytellers are able to wrap a powerful argument in a seamless narrative. Herodotus told the story of Thermopylae because he wanted to persuade the Athenians that the Spartans had fought bravely in defence of a united Greece. He also wanted to illustrate the superiority of the Greeks, who were willing to die for their liberty, over the Persians, who had to whip their troops to make them fight.[58]

Chronology and Causation

A historical narrative uses time to give structure to the past. For this reason, narratives have some obvious chronological features: a beginning, a middle, and an end. This may seem simple, but in the hands of a skilled historian a narrative's events do not simply follow one another: early events are not included just because they happened; they are included because they are related in some significant way to subsequent events.

If you are crafting a narrative, your first task will be to place important events in chronological order. Establishing a chronology is not just an exercise: it helps you to understand change over time. This is vital to understanding the causes of things, and it is not as easy as you might think. For example, historians writing about the Crusades draw on accounts by both Muslims and Christians. Unfortunately, the two religious traditions follow different calendars, which means that the dates of one must be translated in order to establish a coherent chronology.

If you don't know the actual date of an event, you will have to find another source that will give you the information you need to place it in relation to another event. Eighteenth-century English parish records, for instance, don't give birth dates—only the dates when children were baptized. If you want to establish an individual's date of birth, you will have to find another source of information on the customs of that particular place in that particular period, one that will tell you how long after birth children were typically baptized. Even if it is not an easy task, establishing a chronology is crucial if you are to understand change over time.

Get a Sense of Change and Continuity

When you have established the sequence of events, you will begin to get a sense of how some things changed over time while others remained the same. Which events were entirely predictable in the context of the times? Which events were unexpected? Might different historical actors have had different perspectives on the same events?

In 1833, the British Parliament passed legislation abolishing the slave trade and calling for the emancipation of all colonial slaves as of 1 August 1834. After more than 30 years of abolitionist activism, a London journalist might have seen the abolition of slavery as inevitable. For a Barbadian slave, however, emancipation very likely came as a dramatic surprise. On the other hand, the change in the conditions of life for the latter might not have been dramatic at all. Throughout the Caribbean, former slaves were not released immediately: they remained bound to their former owners as apprentices for varying lengths of time. And once the apprenticeship phase had run its course, the land and capital required for sugar production remained out of reach for most, if not all, former slaves. Thus many had no choice but to continue working for their former owners. In that respect, then, former slaves might have experienced more continuity than change.[59]

Select the Participants You Want to Focus On

If you were telling a narrative of emancipation in Barbados, you could focus on former slaves and masters. Or you could choose a narrower focus: slave women who became entrepreneurs, or previously freed townsmen, or colonial bankers, or government officials. Don't forget that your story must make an argument. Do certain individuals illustrate your argument better than others? Were some people more significant agents of change than others? You might decide to exclude some people from your narrative altogether, or leave them in the background and bring others to the front of the stage.

Find Your Own Voice as a Narrator

It may take you some time and experimentation to discover your own narrative voice. Every historian does this differently, but one rule always applies: every narrator must be as faithful as possible to the people and events of the past.

The omniscient narrator. Some historians choose to remain in the background and tell their story from the perspective of an omniscient outsider. Jonathan F. Vance uses this style of narration in his book, *Unlikely Soldiers*, an account of Ken Macalister and Frank Pickersgill, two Canadians who became spies, parachuted into Europe to fight for the French Resistance, and eventually died in a concentration camp during the Second World War. Here he tells the story of their arrival with other prisoners at Buchenwald camp, a

> world into which the thirty-seven agents were transported, to join over 82,000 others in a battle for their very lives. The struggle began as soon as they left the train and were marched along the Caracho Way, named by the prisoners after their slang word for "double time." For the newcomers, the experience was surreal. Despite the hour, the August heat was still oppressive. A few bare light bulbs cast dismal shadows around the perimeter wire; the stars and moon

should have made for a bright summer night sky, but an almost un-natural gloom lay over the camp. Just as stifling was the silence. The guards' rifle butts kept the prisoners quiet, so the only sounds were the occasional wail of a dog and the faint buzz of the electrified fence. It seemed as if they had entered the city of the dead.[60]

> **TIP!** It is your job to inform your readers, not to entertain them, but you don't want to bore them either. Avoid overly dramatic language, but do think about telling your story in an engaging way.

The uncertain narrator. Not all historians approve of omniscient narration, however, and not all sources are reliable enough to permit it. (One might wonder whether the night of prisoner transport in the example above was indeed clear, for instance.) When source materials are so scarce or ambiguous that speculation is required to fill in the gaps, it's best to make those limitations explicit to readers from the start, particularly if the gaps concern significant points.

John Demos uses this strategy in his book *The Unredeemed Captive*, the story of Eunice Williams, a child who was captured by Mohawks in the Deerfield Massacre of 1704. After her abduction, Eunice adapted to the ways of the Kahnawake Iroquois. This disturbed her family but it did not stop them from trying to bring her back to Massachusetts. The information available to Demos was extremely limited, consisting mainly of the letters and diaries of Eunice's English relatives. The family spent decades trying to learn about Eunice, but in the end they recorded very little information. Demos struggles to extract meaning from these scarce sources, but his narrative is at its most compelling when he incorporates quotations from them into his text:

Different it [Eunice's new "style of life"] was, very different. And yet, within a relatively short time, it took. By 1707, Eunice was reported to be "unwilling to return." And the Indians—including, one would presume, her new family—"would as soon part with their hearts" as with this successfully "planted" child.[61]

Choose Your Own Beginning and End

In real life, events are so interconnected across chronological and geographical boundaries that it may be impossible to identify either a beginning or an end. Yet every narrative must have both. Vance begins his story of the Canadian spies with a description of Canadian Ambassador Major-General George Vanier's efforts in 1945 to investigate reports that Canadians had died in concentration camps:

> The major-general had seen more than his fair share of gruesome sights in the trenches of the Western Front, but the studied and technical brutality of the camp appalled him. The cheaply built wooden barracks were lined with bunks, but they were little more than shelves on which the inmates awaited death by disease, starvation, or execution. The Nazis had built electric lifts to raise bodies from the killing chambers to the furnaces to be cremated; blackened human remains still lay in the ovens, and the fact that the crematoria couldn't keep up with the executioners was confirmed by the stacks of rotting corpses piled outside, a few handfuls of lime tossed on to keep down the stench.[62]

Vance is not telling this grisly story just for effect, or to shock his readers. He is setting the scene for a difficult tale of heroism, futility, betrayal, and death. He is preparing his readers for what is to come and placing his story firmly into the context of the Second World War.

Vance sets his opening scene in postwar Buchenwald because this is where the story of the spies reached its end—this is where they died. Looking at their story allows Vance to make some much wider comments about the failure of a major Allied spy operation and about both sides' conduct of the war. Similarly, his story ends not just with the deaths of Macalister and Pickersgill, but with a discussion of what went wrong, in particular how the Physician spy network failed:

> [T]he collapse would never have been as serious or as complete without some major blunders. Had Physician's inner circle

> **TIP!** Notice how Vance uses narrative as a way to analyze what happened. A story without analysis is simply a story. Always ask: what does it mean and why does it matter?

observed basic security precautions, had there been more wireless operators so a few people didn't have to handle so much traffic, had Physician not taken on so many contaminated résistants from Autogiro and Carte—any of these measures would have contained or even prevented the worst of the damage. But [spymaster] Buckmaster's staff must be held accountable for the biggest blunder: the repeated failure to observe the security system of bluff and true checks…. F Section persistently ignored the security measures it drilled into wireless operators. To find the reasons behind the disaster in human weakness rather than in a carefully engineered, high-level plot may not be terribly satisfying in our conspiracy-addicted culture, but it is much more convincing.[63]

Vance ends his narrative here, with a consideration of the context in which Macalister and Pickersgill lived and died. In fact they had been compromised almost from the first moment of their mission, and their handlers then made a series of serious mistakes. In choosing to end here, Vance reminds his readers that this is not simply a story of two brave men who lost their lives in the fight against Nazism, but the story of wider networks, the story of many hundreds of men and women who went "behind the lines," perhaps to suffer similar fates, and the story of how war was—and is—conducted not only on battlefields but also elsewhere. Keep his example in mind when you are constructing a historical narrative: choose a beginning and an end that suit the story you want to tell and the argument you want to make.

REVIEW

1. Use anecdotes to make deliberate points.
2. Include causes and consequences.
3. Control your materials: pick the characters and events you need to make your argument.

Writing Sentences

Historians, like all writers, want to communicate their ideas effectively. They differ from other writers, however, in some of the conventions they follow to achieve this goal. The differences can be confusing for writers trained in other disciplines. But no historical convention is arbitrary: all of them help to ensure that historians' representations of the past are as faithful as possible.

Choose Precise Verbs

At the heart of the sentence is the verb that carries the action. Precise verbs are virtually always preferable to vague ones. What is a vague verb? The most common is the verb "to be"—"is," "are," "was," and so on. These words are indispensable, as the last few sentences show. But beginning writers tend to overuse them—a habit that makes for a dull, lifeless style. It's true that "Alexander Graham Bell was the inventor of the telephone," but you could make the same point more directly if you used the verb that corresponds to the noun "inventor." "Alexander Graham Bell invented the telephone" is more succinct and sounds more lively and natural. In the same way, you could write "There was a large crowd at the meeting," but "A large crowd attended the meeting" sounds better. If you find yourself using a verb of being, try to think of a more precise, active alternative.

> **TIP!** Apply this idea to all your words and ideas—be precise. Don't just say that Pierre Trudeau was a good (or poor) prime minister—show the specific reasons for your opinion. Choose all of your words carefully.

Make Passive Sentences Active

One of the main goals of historical writing is to uncover who did what. It follows that one of the worst things a historian can do is to obscure that information. Too often, that is exactly what the passive voice does. In fact, passive constructions can obliterate historical actors altogether: "New France was surrendered in September 1760." By whom? To whom? If you can't state with certainty that "Governor Vaudreuil surrendered New France to General Amherst in September 1760," then you may well be confused. At the very least, you owe your readers an explanation.

As you read more history, you may notice that the passive is often a sign of weak reasoning or insufficient information. This is not necessarily the case in other disciplines. Until quite recently, for instance, use of the passive was standard in the natural sciences, which sought to downplay individuals' personal involvement in research and emphasize the objectivity of their work. One of the biggest challenges for historians of science today is to cut through the passive prose and find out not just what was done, but who did it.

There are times when the passive can't be avoided. In some circumstances it is even appropriate: the preceding sentence would have been less direct if it had read "There are times when historians can't avoid using the passive." The best writers will occasionally use passive constructions. Nevertheless, the passive can confuse the order of ideas and should be used sparingly.

Use the Past Tense

Historians rarely write in the present tense. This is hardly surprising. If you are discussing events that took place in the past, it makes sense to use the past tense. It also helps to ensure that you keep those events in an intelligible chronological order

It is conventional for scholars of literature to write about authors and their works in the present tense. Thus a literary critic discussing the work of the novelist Suzanne Desrochers might write that "Desrochers writes evocatively about the experiences of young

French women sent to New France in the 1660s as prospective brides for French settlers," and a literature instructor would probably use the present tense when discussing Desrochers's use of language. By contrast, a historian analyzing Desrochers' work—perhaps as a way to understand her experience as a French Canadian—would use the past tense to discuss the author herself: "Brought up in the Ontario Francophone community of Lafontaine, on Georgian Bay, Desrochers was much influenced by the work of her aunt, who traced the family's Canadian roots to the early 1600s." Using the present tense might confuse the chronology of Desrochers's life and experiences, but using the past tense makes it possible to locate events clearly in relationship to one another.

The present tense is appropriate, however—even for a historian—when discussing fictional characters or events. Similarly, historians use the present tense when writing about contemporary work or living scholars.

> **TIP!** A word on verb forms: "he did it" (past), "he had done it" (further in the past), "he would have done it" (past but uncertain). Notice that the verb form is "would have," not "would of." This is a very common error.

Try to Avoid Split Infinitives

In English, the infinitive is the form of the verb accompanied by the preposition "to," as in "to go," "to walk," or "to be or not to be." It is the most basic form, unattached to any subject or object.

For generations, teachers insisted that the infinitive should never be "split" by placing an adverb between "to" and the verb, as in the famous *Star Trek* line "To boldly go where no one has gone before." Today most grammarians agree that split infinitives are very common in spoken English, and that there are times when placing the adverb anywhere else would alter the meaning of the sentence. There are also times when a split infinitive simply sounds better. If the *Star*

Trek writers had put their adverb in the "correct" place, the line would have been "To go boldly..." How uninspiring.

In general, though, historians still try to avoid splitting infinitives, if only because so many people consider it a serious grammatical error. If repositioning the adverb would change your meaning or create an awkward, unnatural rhythm, you may be able to recast the sentence.

Write Complete Sentences

In principle, a sentence is a sentence only if it has both a subject (noun) and a predicate (verb), and yet there are times when a phrase with neither can be appropriate (as in the case of the "How uninspiring" comment above). Incomplete sentences can add punch and colour to informal writing, but they really do not have a place in formal historical writing. If you do use an incomplete sentence in a work of history, you should be very sure that readers will understand your intent and know that you are indeed in control of your own writing: otherwise they will simply assume that your grammar is not up to scratch.

Put Your Ideas in an Intelligible Order

You must put your ideas in an order that your readers will understand. This is not as easy as it sounds. After weeks of reading and research, you will have become so steeped in your topic that the complex connections between the people, ideas, and events you are writing about will seem perfectly obvious to you. Now it is your job to unravel those complexities and place your ideas in a sequence of words. In each sentence, you must imagine what your readers need to know first, second, and third. Reread every sentence you write and ask yourself whether it would be totally clear to someone else. Unless your professor instructs you otherwise, you should assume that you're writing for an intelligent reader who is generally well informed, but has no specific knowledge of your topic area.

Keep Related Words Together

"The tail-gunner saw a cloud form over Hiroshima in the shape of a mushroom." This sentence likely makes perfect sense to you because you have seen pictures of the infamous mushroom cloud. Imagine, though, if you spoke that sentence to someone who had never seen such a picture. That person would have to rely on the sequence of the words to grasp your meaning, and in this case the sequence would be baffling. After all, it isn't Hiroshima that has the shape of the mushroom: it's the cloud. Your point would be clearer if you kept related words close together: "The tail-gunner saw a mushroom-shaped cloud form over Hiroshima." If you keep related words together, readers won't have to pause at the end of the sentence to figure out what it meant.

Make Sure that Pronoun References are Clear

By definition, a pronoun substitutes for a noun. For a pronoun to make sense, however, readers have to be able to tell which noun it replaces, and they can't do that unless you have taken care to avoid any possible ambiguity. You know in your head which pronoun refers to which noun, but your readers must infer the relationship from the way you place the words. Consider this sentence: "John A. Macdonald's 1864 partnership with George Brown demonstrated his political practicality and flexibility." Does "his" refer to Macdonald or to Brown? A reader might infer that, since "his" is closer to "Brown," the practicality and flexibility are Brown's. But this may not be your meaning. Both Brown and Macdonald were talented politicians, and both could be described as practical and flexible. There are several ways of recasting the sentence to avoid such confusion: "John A. Macdonald demonstrated political practicality and flexibility in his 1864 partnership with George Brown" or "John A. Macdonald's 1864 partnership with George Brown demonstrated his own political practicality and flexibility"; or even "John A. Macdonald's 1864 partnership with George Brown demonstrated

Brown's political practicality and flexibility." In each case, a minor adjustment will create a much clearer sentence.

Keep Subjects and Verbs Close Together

The principal relationship in a sentence is between the subject and the verb. In general, it's best not to put too much information between them. Take a look at this sentence: "Grey Owl, after two years with the Canadian army in the First World War, spent his life as a hunter, guide, and conservationist." As a reader, you have to hold "Grey Owl" in the back of your mind until you find out what he is doing. The idea would be clearer if you wrote that "After two years with the Canadian army in the First World War, Grey Owl spent his life as a hunter, guide, and conservationist." It's usually acceptable to place a short phrase between a subject and verb, however: "Grey Owl, born Archie Belaney, spent his life as a hunter, guide, and conservationist."

> **TIP!** It's all about clarity—don't assume that your readers will automatically know what you mean.

Begin on Common Ground and Move towards a New Point

A sentence is not just a series of words arranged in an orderly fashion. In history, as in all writing, a sentence develops an idea that has already been established (usually, though not necessarily, in the preceding sentence) and develops it so as to carry the reader in a certain direction. In other words, a sentence does not function in isolation: it needs to connect in some way with the sentences on either side of it. Consider this sequence of sentences:

> Mackenzie King was particularly devoted to his dog Pat I. He had three Irish terriers, all of which were named Pat. After Pat I died, King tried to communicate with his spirit.

Here the reader has to jump from a specific statement about one of King's dogs to a general statement about all of them and then back to another specific statement. A better sequence would move from the general to the specific:

> Mackenzie King had three Irish terriers, all of which were named Pat. He was particularly devoted to Pat I. After Pat I died, King tried to communicate with his spirit.

In this sequence, the connections between the sentences are smooth.

Put the Emphasis at the End

If you are developing your ideas over the course of a sentence, then the end of the sentence should be interesting and emphatic. One master of emphatic writing (and speaking) was Winston Churchill. Here is what Churchill wrote about the Crusades in his book *The Birth of Britain*:

> The Crusading spirit had for some time stirred the minds of men all over western Europe. The Christian kingdoms of Spain had led the way with their holy wars against the Arabs. Now, towards the end of the eleventh century, a new enemy of Christendom appeared fifteen hundred miles to the east. The Seljuk Turks were pressing hard upon the Byzantine Empire in Asia Minor, and harassing devout pilgrims from Europe through Syria to the Holy Land.[64]

Notice how each sentence begins with a connection to the previous sentence. Also notice how each sentence develops in a new direction and concludes with a new idea. The second sentence is especially skillful. It begins by saying something specific about the western European Christians, but then leads readers to consider the Christians' enemies, the Arabs.

Use Parallel Forms for Emphasis

One of the best tricks for writing an effective sentence is to use a parallel construction, expressing related ideas in a similar grammatical form. On 8 October 1940, as Nazi bombers were pounding Britain, Churchill told the House of Commons that "Death and sorrow will be the companions of our journey; hardship our garment; constancy and valour our only shield. We must be united, we must be undaunted, we must be inflexible."[65] He constructed the first sentence loosely around the repetition of "our"; then he constructed the second sentence tightly around the repetition of "we must be." In a parallel construction, parallel ideas are expressed in a parallel grammatical structure and each adds weight to the whole construction.

Break the Rules if You Must

As valuable as all these conventions may be, there are times when strict observance could force you to write an ugly, unnatural sentence. In such cases, break the rules. Good historical writers understand the spirit of the law as well as the letter. Your first task is to get your meaning across, and to do it persuasively.

REVIEW

1. Think! Make every word and every sentence count.
2. Pay special attention to verbs.
3. Use word order to your advantage.

Choosing Words

In history as in life, word choice can make all the difference. The past abounds with catastrophic examples of poorly chosen or even deliberately misleading words. One example is the 1840 Treaty of Waitangi, in which the British took New Zealand from the Maoris by mistranslating the word for "sovereignty."[66] This deliberate act of imprecision has caused a century and a half of bad feelings. Get into the habit of checking your essays for diction. The basic rules of diction often strike inexperienced writers as arbitrary. They are not.

Be Concise

Some people seem to think that the best way to impress readers with the complexity of their ideas is to use as many words as possible to express them. They are wrong. Readers will be more impressed if you make every word count. If "It is an undeniable fact that William the Conqueror was instrumental in establishing the Norman regime," why not simply state the fact? "William the Conqueror established the Norman regime." Why use 16 words to say something that you could say in 7? If you can resist the temptation to cram your paper with unnecessary words, readers will thank you for not straining their patience.

> **TIP!** Believe it or not, it can be more difficult to write a short paper than a long one. If your page limit is severely limited, check every sentence to see if you can shorten it by changing or omitting a few words.

Avoid Jargon

Most historians try to use language that non-specialist readers will understand. This tendency sets history apart from several of its fellow social sciences. Disciplines such as anthropology, economics, political science, and sociology each have their own **jargon**: a specialized language that helps people within the field communicate but tends to shut everyone else out. History doesn't have its own private language, but sometimes historians will borrow jargon from other fields. For example, *The Canadian Oxford Dictionary* defines "hegemony" as "leadership esp. by one state of a confederacy," but professional historians associate the term with a Marxist philosopher and political theorist named Antonio Gramsci, who used it in the sense of social power or dominance. If you are writing for historians, you can expect them to understand the term as you do, but to a wider audience "hegemony" may be incomprehensible jargon. When in doubt, either use ordinary language or be sure to define your terms carefully.

Awkward jargon from the legal profession can also slip into historical writing. Legal documents are written for a specific audience (the court) and purpose (to protect the interests of the lawyer's client). Lawyers use archaic terminology, repetition, and formal terms like "the said," "party to the first part," and "stipulate." This kind of language should be used only by lawyers, for lawyers. It has no place in a history paper, unless you are writing about an actual court case and need to quote from the proceedings. Otherwise, use plain English.

Perhaps even less appropriate for historical writing is government jargon, sometimes known as "officialese." This is the awkward, abstract, often pompous language that many politicians and bureaucrats learn to use to protect themselves, avoid precise commitments, or make themselves sound important. In his famous essay "Politics and the English Language," George Orwell imagined how a bureaucrat might translate the following passage from the Bible (Ecclesiastes 9:11):

> I returned and saw under the sun, that the race is not to the swift, nor the battle to the strong, neither yet bread to the wise, nor yet

riches to men of understanding, nor yet favour to men of skill; but time and chance happeneth to them all.

Here is Orwell's translation:

Objective consideration of contemporary phenomena compels the conclusion that success or failure in competitive activities exhibits no tendency to be commensurate with innate capacity, but that a considerable element of the unpredictable must invariably be taken into account.[67]

Orwell's point is clear: the pretentious, abstract language of the bureaucratic "translation" is no match for the clean, simple words, natural rhythms, and concrete imagery of the original passage.

Avoid Both Pretentious and Colloquial Language

Don't count on big, complicated words to make you look smart or sound appropriately formal. You will sound pretentious and may confuse or annoy your readers. You may want to argue that central planning had a "procrustean" effect on Soviet engineering, but if your readers don't know that the word refers to a ruthless insistence on uniformity, they will have no idea what you are talking about. Even if they do know the word, it's likely to stand out from the rest of your writing and sound out of place. Control the urge to show off: use only words that you are comfortable with. Similarly, avoid the temptation to quote impressive-sounding words and passages from your sources unless you will discuss them clearly—otherwise, your reader may suspect that you do not understand the complex material properly yourself.

On the other hand, most history instructors will expect you to write in formal English. This means that you should avoid slang, contractions ("isn't," "doesn't," "it's"), and an overly casual tone, except as part of a quotation. Such informal or **colloquial language** is fine in many other types of writing (such as this guide), but it does not belong in formal academic writing. Aim to use language precisely and carefully: remember that your reader cannot fill in the blanks and has no idea what is in your head. What is on paper must say it all, so make sure that you are saying exactly what you want to say and that you are expressing your meaning clearly.

Choose Words Thoughtfully

Be Sensitive to Political Issues

Historical writing has always reflected the politics of the times. Today historians are particularly sensitive to language that could be perceived as discriminatory or "politically incorrect." Conservatives may complain that liberals are forcing "linguistic engineering" on them; liberals, that conservatives have not gone far enough to purge their language of words that may cause offence. The dispute will never be resolved, but everyone can agree that writers who want to communicate need to be aware of how their readers will respond to their language.

Racial designations in particular have changed considerably over recent decades. "Negro" and "coloured" changed to "black," which was then increasingly replaced by "African-American," "African-Canadian," and so on. Another term that was once common is "Oriental"—we would now say "Asian." We would use the terms "Global North" and "Global South" rather than "Third World."

In Canada, "Indian" has been largely replaced by "First Nations" in the case of organized bands or communities, although "Indian" is still required in some legal contexts, particularly those that connect to the federal Indian Acts. In broader contexts, especially those that include Metis and Inuit people, "Aboriginal" and "Native" are fine so long as you use them as adjectives (as in "Aboriginal people" or "Native traditions"), but they should not be used as nouns. If you are writing about a particular group, nation, or band (a unit of administration), you should always use its specific name. You should also be aware that modern terms and classifications do not necessarily coincide with historic realities. Some First Nations people, for example, point out that the concept of the "nation" itself is not indigenous to their societies; it is a European concept that was introduced to them relatively recently. Finally, note that what is considered "correct" in terms of titles and spellings may be a subject of debate and change; try to be informed about such debates and sensitive to them. Whenever possible, call people by the names they call themselves.

Be Sensitive to Gender Issues

In the 1890s Oscar Wilde said, "Anybody can make history. Only a great man can write it." His point was to call attention to the challenge of writing history well, but people today could be forgiven if they were distracted from it by the apparent sexism of the phrase "great man." It's quite possible that Wilde had no intention of ruling out the idea of a great woman historian. But he was a man of his time, and at that time "man" meant (among other things) "human" or "person."

In recent years historians have become more sensitive to gender. This is reflected not only in their intellectual interests but also in their historical writing. Years ago it was acceptable to say, for example, "The historian must analyze sources. He must understand the relevant documents." The use of the masculine pronoun to refer to a noun of indeterminate gender was conventional. Fortunately, there are plenty of female historians today—so many that Wilde's statement now seems not only biased but inaccurate.

To avoid such sexist pitfalls, you may be tempted to use keyboard gymnastics: "He/she must understand the relevant documents," or, "S/he must understand. . ." These slashed pronouns are awkward constructions, and rather distracting to read. Luckily, they are usually easy to avoid. First, consider using neutral pronouns like "everyone," "anybody," and "everybody." If that doesn't work, you can often turn a singular into a plural: "Historians must analyze sources. They must understand the relevant documents." Changing a gender-specific singular to a gender-neutral plural conveys the same idea without any sexist overtones.

You might also be tempted to substitute the third-person-singular neutral pronoun "one" for a gender-biased "he." "When one is a historian, one must analyze sources." This construction is grammatically correct, but it sounds pretentious today.

While we are on the subject of gender-neutral language, it's worth noting one other common problem: the word "mankind." An easy way around this one is simply to substitute "people" or "humankind," whichever suits your meaning more precisely.

TIP! Watch out for any tendency to judge historical people in today's terms: think long and hard before using terms like "primitive" or "backwards." People today are not more intelligent than people in the past.

Avoid Euphemisms

"Politically correct" language is sometimes necessary to avoid giving offence, but it can often seem silly or evasive, if not downright deceitful. If you describe people you believe to be stupid as "intellectually challenged," you are using a **euphemism**: a polite term designed to disguise a harsh reality, and probably an insult. The twentieth century seems to have been especially rich in euphemisms: torched villages were "pacified," totalitarian regimes were "people's republics," and the massacre of one ethnic group by another was a matter of "cleansing." In general, it's best to say what you really mean. When you come across a euphemism, it's also a good idea to ask yourself whose interest it really serves.

Choose Figurative Language Carefully

When you are writing about a subject that might be unfamiliar to your readers, it sometimes helps to make an imaginative comparison with something else that your readers are likely to know—in other words, to use a simile or a metaphor. It would be perfectly acceptable to write "Mahatma Gandhi took part in the decolonization movement of India." It would be better to use a slightly more informative metaphor: "Mahatma Gandhi played a leading role in the decolonization movement of India." It might be even more effective to say that "Mahatma Gandhi was the Nelson Mandela of India," although you might have to sustain the metaphor by specifying the respects in which they resembled one another. Metaphors and similes add colour to historical writing, but it takes practice to use them well.

Use Metaphors and Similes Judiciously

There are several ways for a metaphor to go awry. Suppose, for instance, that you had described Gandhi as "the Nicolás Bravo of India" For one thing, chances are that most people reading an essay on Indian history would never have heard of Bravo, a conservative politician who led a rebellion against the president of Mexico in 1827–8. But the comparison is hopelessly flawed in any case because Bravo's armed revolution failed while Gandhi's political one succeeded. Metaphors and similes can add vitality to your writing, but only if they make sense to your readers.

Avoid Clichés

Readers generally welcome colourful language, but they will find your colours boring if they are introduced for no particular reason or are too predictable. Colourful expressions that have been overused are called **clichés**. Replace them with plain language or less predictable metaphors.

There is a simple test you can use to spot a cliché. If you can remove the last word from a phrase and still be sure that readers will be able to fill it in, you are looking at a cliché:

- "Queen Elizabeth did not suffer fools . . . (gladly)."
- "Albert Einstein burned the midnight . . . (oil)."
- "The bubonic plague reared its ugly . . . (head)."

> **TIP!** Try to avoid big, general statements like "everyone knows that..." or "People have always...." These statements don't generally mean much and are easy to challenge: how can you possibly prove that they are true?

Don't Use Unfamiliar Foreign Words

Historians often use foreign words or expressions. Some foreign terms have come into common English usage, as in "Trudeau was a politician *par excellence*," or "The right of *habeas corpus* is fundamental to Canadian law." When you write about a foreign culture, however, you should be careful with foreign terms.

The rule of thumb is to use only terms that your audience will understand. Imagine that you were writing about the history of the amaXhosa, a people of southern Africa. If the class were a seminar on southern African history and your instructor was a specialist in the field, it might well be appropriate for you to spell out the name "amaXhosa." This is because a specialist in southern African history would know that these people form the plural of their collective name by adding the prefix "ama." If you were writing for a more general audience—say, in a survey of world history—you probably wouldn't want to bother explaining the linguistic intricacies. In that case the best choice might be to refer to your subjects as "the Xhosa," a compromise that would let readers know you were savvy enough not to apply the English rule for forming plurals to a foreign word. It's important to know your readers and to meet them on common ground.

> **TIP!** Make sure that your readers will understand your allusions—for example, to compare a nineteenth-century popular musician with Iggy Azalea or Drake is probably not going to have a lot of meaning for the typical history professor. If you know that your professor is a fan of rap music, on the other hand, then this allusion might work very well.

Check for Common Diction Problems

It's easy to misuse words and expressions, especially ones that are often misused or misunderstood. If you suspect that you may have misused one of the following words or phrases in an essay, run a search on your computer to find it. Then consult your dictionary to make sure you have used it correctly.

If you need further assistance on points of usage, ask a reference librarian to help you find *The New Fowler's Modern English Usage*, ed. R.W. Burchfield (Oxford: Oxford University Press, 2004). The updated version of H.W. Fowler's classic work on English usage, it is the basis for many of the entries in the following list of common problems in historical writing:

AD and **BC** are abbreviations meaning *Anno Domini* ("the year of our Lord") and "Before Christ." Increasingly, they are being replaced by the non-religious abbreviations BCE and CE, meaning "Before Common Era" and "Common Era" respectively. When you think about it, the new abbreviations don't really change much, but they are increasingly popular. Whichever one you decide to use, be consistent.

Accept and **except** have very different meanings. "Accept" is a verb that means to receive or agree to something, while "except" is a preposition indicating that something is excluded or omitted. To keep the words separate in your mind, you might find it helpful to link except with exclude.

Affect and **effect** confuse many students, but they are quite easy to differentiate. "Affect" is most often used as a verb meaning "to act upon": for example, hunger might affect one's mood. "Effect," on the other hand, is usually a noun referring to a result: one effect of a bad mood might be that you snap at your roommate.

All right is proper for formal writing. Many people spell it as "alright," but most authorities regard "alright" as overly casual. It's not all right to write "alright" in a formal essay.

All together and **altogether** do not mean the same thing. "All together" expresses a complete group, while "altogether" means completely or entirely. Here is a sentence to make the difference clear. "We are going to the hockey game all together, but I am not altogether sure that it's a good idea."

And/or appears frequently in insecure writing, possibly because it has a legalistic sound to it. "And/or" is not incorrect, but it is awkward and usually unnecessary. You can avoid it by substituting "X or Y or both" or even a simple "or."

Ante- and **anti-** are two Latin prefixes that students often confuse. "Ante" means *before*, while "anti" means *against*. For example, "antebellum America" refers to the period before the American Civil War, whereas "antiwar protestors" opposed the war.

Apart and **a part** also often confuse students, but they mean very different things: "I took a part of the bun and tore that apart." If you can substitute with the words "a portion," then you need the two separate words, "a part."

Because is a common word in historical writing, because historians are often seeking to explain what caused something to happen: "Letitia Youmans founded the first Canadian local of the Women's Christian Temperance Union because she was distressed by the effects of alcohol on family life." Elementary-school teachers tell students not to start a sentence with "because," and in general they are right to do so. "Because" introduces a clause that depends on another clause; if you reversed the order of the two clauses about Youmans, the sentence would be harder to follow. You need to know the effect (that is, what has happened) before you can really take in the cause (the reason why). Still, there are circumstances when it is reasonable to make an exception to the rule.

Bias and **biased** cause all sorts of trouble for students, who often write phrases such as "he was bias." "Bias" is a noun, however, and it denotes a preference: "Vaudreuil had a bias towards guerrilla warfare techniques." "Biased," on the other hand, is an adjective: "Vaudreuil was biased in favour of guerrilla warfare techniques rather than pitched battles." Please note that since all of us have preferences, all of us have biases and there is nothing wrong with this as long as we are aware of our biases and don't let them unduly affect our work.

In the discipline of history, however, if the word "biased" is used as a criticism then it describes an unreasonable or unfair preference or an opinion that is so fixed it defies evidence and reason: "Hitler was biased against Jews."

Border and **boarder** have nothing to do with each other, but can easily confuse writers. When we are talking of geopolitical divisions, we are talking of borders: "Canadians often cross the border to shop in the United States." Boarders, on the other hand, are people who pay for meals and lodging in other people's homes: "I am a boarder at the Smiths' house this semester."

Cannot is usually written as one word, not two ("can not"). "Can't" is a contraction, inappropriate in academic writing.

Complement and **compliment** can easily confuse students. When we say something pleasant to someone, we may be paying them a compliment: "Your speech was very interesting." Complement can have several meanings, but it always refers to things that go well together: "Jim Flaherty's talents as a finance minister complemented Stephen Harper's style of diplomacy."

Different is the subject of some debate. Real sticklers will tell you that "different" can be followed only by "from," never by "than" or "to." The editors of *The Oxford English Dictionary* disagree. They say that people have been using "different to" since 1526 and "different than" since 1644. Is it possible that so many people could be so wrong for so long? Perhaps. Somehow, "different from" still sounds better.

Double negatives are not uncommon in historical writing, but they should be used sparingly. Two negatives always cancel each other out: "John A. MacDonald was not displeased by the result of the vote" is a roundabout way of saying that he was at least somewhat pleased. Occasionally a double negative can add an ironic note (as in the first sentence above), but a straightforward positive is usually best.

Due to might seem harmless enough, but generations of history professors have warned students against it. Strunk and White, in their classic *The Elements of Style*, explain that "due to" should be used only to mean "attributable to," as in "Custer's defeat was due to poor intelligence." It should not substitute for "because" or "through," as in "Custer lost the battle due to poor intelligence."

Into and **in to** are not interchangeable. "Into" is the word you want when you are talking about motion ("She walked into the meeting"), direction ("He looked into her eyes"), or a change of condition or state: ("A caterpillar turns into a butterfly"; "The group separated into factions"; "The marchers broke into song"). Sometimes, however, "in" and "to" are completely separate. For example, in the sentence "The troops moved in to surround the rebels," the "in" is part of the verbal phrase "moved in," while the "to" is part of the infinitive "to surround." In other cases the "to" may be a simple preposition: "He turned the umbrella in to the lost and found."

It's and **its** get confused frequently, even though they mean two completely different things. "It's" is the contraction of "it is": "It's not too late to learn how to write history." "Its" is the possessive form of "it": "When Castro lit a Montecristo, its pungent smoke filled the air." (It's worth remembering that, since "it's" is a contraction, it should not appear in academic writing anyway.)

Lead and **led** also are confused frequently. "Lead" can mean two different things that can easily be distinguished in the context of a sentence: it can refer to a metallic element (a lead weight, for instance) or it is the present tense of the verb "to lead" ("I will lead you towards the path.") The past tense of "to lead" is "led" ("She led the horse to the stable.") Please notice the spelling on the past tense, which is where most mistakes are made.

Led to. It may be true that the First World War led to the Second World War: just don't confuse chronology with causation. The events of 1939 certainly followed those of 1914, but does that mean that they were caused by them? "Led to" will lead your readers to expect an explanation of how the first war helped to cause the second.

Lie and **lay** cause a lot of trouble. Generally speaking, to "lie" in the physical sense means to lie down, as in "lie down on a bed." "Lay," on the other hand, means to place something, as in "lay down a heavy load." We lie down when we are tired, but first we lay down whatever we have been carrying. The confusion probably arises because "lay" is also the past tense of "lie" ("I lay down on the couch for a nap and two minutes later the phone rang").

Lifestyle is an imprecise modern term that has no place in historical writing. The following sentence comes from a student essay: "The lifestyle of the African-American slaves cannot be compared with the lifestyle of the concentration camp inmates." It's unlikely that either of those groups ever had a lifestyle. The writer would have done better to refer to their living conditions or their experiences.

Maybe and **may be** are not interchangeable, although both express doubt or uncertainty. The two words "may be" is a verb form: "I may be going home in December." The single word "maybe," on the other hand, is an adverb that expresses possibility: "Maybe I'll go home in December." If you can substitute the word "perhaps" and the sentence still makes sense, you want to use "maybe."

Native is a dangerous word in historical writing. You could refer to "the native Tahitians" just as you might refer to "the native French." But you should never refer to either group as "the natives." "Natives" is a term that Europeans once reserved for people from other parts of the world whom they deemed to be uncivilized. Today that kind of derogatory language is not tolerated. By contrast, the adjective "Native" (with a capital "N") is widely accepted, along with "Aboriginal" (as long as it's capitalized and used as an adjective).

People is a deceptively simple word that is easy to misuse. It can refer to a group of human beings who share some characteristic:

"Aboriginal people made up 3.8 per cent of Canada's population in 2006." It can also refer to those who belong to a state or nation: "Aboriginal peoples such as the Cree and the Ojibway are struggling to preserve their languages." In the same way, we refer to the specific European peoples, such as the French or the Germans, and also to European people more generally.

Principal and **principle** can be quite confusing. "Principal" is an adjective that refers to the first or the most important: for example, the principal dancer in a ballet company, or the principal points of an argument. "Principle," on the other hand, is a noun referring to a general law, a rule or a standard: for instance, the principle of equal pay for equal work.

Regard is misused frequently in expressions such as "with regards to" and "in regards to." There are two proper ways to use "regard." If it is a noun (part of a compound preposition), use the singular: "with regard to" or "in regard to." If it is a verb, conjugate accordingly: "as it regards" or "as they regard."

Role and **roll** mean totally different things, but students often mix them up. In history, role is more common: "Stalin took advantage of his role as Party Secretary in order to gain complete control of the Communist party." "Roll," on the other hand, refers to baked goods and movement: "Rover's trick was to roll over—if he did it successfully, Joe gave him a piece of a roll."

That and **which** have been the subject of considerable confusion among historians and other writers. In the following sentences, which one would you use?

1. "The tariffs *that/which* came to be known as the Corn Laws were repealed in 1846.
2. "The Corn Laws, *that/which* had protected English farmers from foreign competition, were repealed in 1846."

If you chose "that" for sentence 1 and "which" for sentence 2, you are correct. In the first sentence, the phrase "that came to be known as the Corn Laws" is restrictive (or defining) because it is essential in order to identify the particular tariffs in question. If you take out the phrase, "that came to be known as the Corn Laws," the sentence would be grammatically correct, but seriously uninformative: what tariffs?

In the second sentence, by contrast, the phrase "which had protected English farmers from foreign competition" is non-restrictive; it is not essential to the meaning of the sentence and therefore is set off by commas. It is simply a little piece of additional explanation, and if you remove the part between the commas, the sentence still makes total sense.

Consistent use of "that" for restrictive and "which" for non-restrictive modifiers does make for a cleaner style. But you may notice that many fine writers do not always follow the rule.

There and **their**. "There" is the adverb ("He worked there for 30 years") and "their" is the possessive pronoun ("She is their representative.") Here is a sentence to show the difference: "In his famous painting of the Fathers of Confederation, Robert Harris paid careful attention to their positioning so as to show that there was a real hierarchy of political importance among them."

To, **too**, and **two** also give many students trouble. The simple "to" is a preposition ("He decided to run for election"; "She was elected to the House of Commons"). "Too" is an adverb with several uses ("This coffee is too hot to drink now"; "Did your brother go too?"). And "two" is the number. They mean completely different things. Here is a sentence that makes the differences clear: "When they went to Montreal, they saw two hockey games and bought too many souvenirs."

Tribe and **tribal** are subject to the same general rules as "Native." A long time ago, anthropologists used "tribe" precisely to refer to a group of people who claim descent from a common ancestor, real or imagined. Unfortunately, some historians and journalists took to using "tribe" loosely and offensively, to refer to any group of people with brown skin. Even today, a conflict that would be described as "ethnic" if it took place in Bosnia is likely to be described as "tribal" if it takes place in Rwanda. This usage derives from efforts of European administrators to classify and regulate the peoples of their former colonies. Ironically, some African and Native American groups took up the practice and now call themselves "tribes."

Were and **where** seem to confuse many students. "Were" is a verb form and "where" is an adverb that usually refers to a place or a situation: "The *filles du roi* were young Frenchwomen whose passage to Canada, where they hoped to find husbands, was sponsored by the king."

Whose and **who's**. "Whose" is the possessive form of the word "who" ("The politician whose speeches were most effective"), while "who's" is a contraction of "who is" ("The politician who's running in the next election.") Since it is not appropriate to use contractions in academic writing, it is surprising to see how often "who's" turns up in student essays.

Your and **you're**. "Your" is the possessive form of the word "you" (Please pick up your paper on Wednesday"), while "you're" is a contraction of "you are" ("You're welcome!") Again, since it is not appropriate to use contractions in academic writing, "you're" should never be used in history essays.

REVIEW

1. Choose your words carefully.
2. Spelling counts!
3. Avoid slang and contractions.
4. Be direct and clear—say what you mean.

PRACTICE EXERCISE

For each of the following sentences, choose the correct word to fill the blank space.

1. When Amor de Cosmos entered BC politics, he attacked the ruling elites and (there/their) _____ privileges.
2. In Canada, conscription was used in (to/two/too) _____ twentieth-century world wars.
3. After a lengthy political debate, (that/which) _____ was quite heated, Canadians rejected the Charlottetown Constitutional Accord.
4. The Red River Resistance of 1869–70 (cannot/can not) _____ be seen as a complete success.
5. It is (all right/alright) _____ to ask questions about referencing methods.
6. In the 1860s, (there/their) _____ were several Fenian raids into Canadian territory.
7. In the 1960s, (ante-/anti-) _____ war sentiment was quite strong in Canada.
8. The principal players in the Nootka Sound Convention of 1790 (were/where) _____ the British and Spanish governments.
9. The Bluenose schooner was first depicted on the dime in 1937, at the height of (its/it's) _____ fame.
10. The Winnipeg General Strike of 1919 had an impact (that/which) _____ was felt across Canada.
11. Labrador was severely (affected/effected) _____ by the Spanish flu epidemic of 1918–19. One (affect/effect) _____ was the loss of more than 25 per cent of its coastal population.
12. Laura Secord, (whose/who's) _____ famous walk to warn British troops about a planned American ambush (lead/led) _____ to an enduring Canadian legend, was born in 1775.
13. In Canada, the (principal/principle) _____ significance of the 1923 Halibut Treaty (lays/lies)_____ in its status as the first international treaty to have been signed by Canadian rather than British statesmen.
14. Canadians (accepted/excepted) _____ the first Official Languages Act in 1969.
15. Every Canadian prime minister (accept/except) _____ Kim Campbell has been male.

continued

16. The Royal North West Mounted Police together with the Dominion Police turned (into/in to) _____ the RCMP.
17. The stolen goods were turned (into/in to) _____ the RCMP.
18. Justin Trudeau (lead/led)_____ the Liberal party to victory in the 2015 election.
19. The disputes between the La Tour and d'Aulnay families tore Acadian society (apart/a part) _____in the 1640s.
20. The loss of New France (maybe/may be)_____ partly attributable to the rivalry between Montcalm and Vaudreuil.

Answer Key

1. their
2. two
3. which
4. cannot
5. all right
6. there
7. anti-
8. were
9. its
10. that
11. affected; effect
12. whose; led
13. principal; lies
14. accepted
15. except
16. into
17. in to
18. led
19. apart
20. may be

Revising and Editing

This guide is not a history cookbook, for the simple reason that there are no recipes for writing history. There are conventions, of course, but every historian has his or her own way of writing. Approaches to any given project depend partly on personal style and partly on the subject of the work. The more you write, the stronger your sense of your own style and interests will become. At the same time, you will become more familiar with your own strengths and weaknesses. You have probably heard of the ancient Greek inscription over the temple at Delphi: "Know thyself." Get to know your weaknesses as a writer, then watch out for them.

Get Some Perspective on Your Draft

Once your draft is completed, it's important to get some distance from it before you begin the revision process. Try to spend a few days working on other things. If you don't have days to spare, even an hour doing something else will help you to see your paper as your readers will, with fresh eyes.

If you're lucky, you may have an instructor or friend who would be willing to read a first draft and comment on it. Take any critical comments seriously. Early comments on a draft can help you determine whether you have made a persuasive case. A critical reader will assess both the strengths and the weaknesses of your paper. Sometimes it is difficult to take criticism, but the best critics spend a great deal of time thinking about your work. This in itself is a compliment. Even if you conclude that some unfavourable comment was mistaken, the criticism will have had the positive effect of making you reconfirm your position.

Think about a Title

Now that you have finalized your argument, you can start thinking about a title. The best titles are not just informative but also intriguing. One student, writing a paper about an ancient Egyptian queen who, on the death of her husband, declared herself king, chose the title "She's the Man: An Analysis of Hatshepsut's Reign." The subtitle alone would have been an adequate title, but the touch of humour made the full version more effective. Another student, writing about the film *Schindler's List*, entitled it "The List Was Life and the List Was Good, but Was the Movie? A Historical Analysis of *Schindler's List*." Again, the subtitle would have been enough, but a bit of a yawn. The full version, with its subtle allusion to the creation story in the Bible, was more likely to catch a reader's attention. In both cases, the title gave some insight into the point of the paper.

> **TIP!** Pay attention to your audience: if you are going to inject a note of humour or informality into your title, be sure that your instructor will accept it. It is possible, after all, to be interesting without being funny.

Revise Your Draft

Now that you have some perspective on your writing, it's time to begin revising. First address your critic's comments, which may concern both the style and the substance of the paper. Write another draft that incorporates the suggested changes. Then stand back and assess the paper again. Have you addressed your critic's comments fully? If not, do you have good reason to reject the comments?

No critic, no matter how generous, will tell you everything you need to know in order to turn your draft into a prize-winning piece of writing. You yourself must take responsibility for revising. One basic strategy is to begin with broad revisions to the arguments and narratives before tackling the details of sentences and word choice. Finally, you will need to proofread for spelling, grammar, punctuation, and formatting.

Evaluate Your Own Arguments and Narratives

The key components of historical argumentation were outlined in Chapter 3. Check your writing thoroughly for the following points. Does the evidence support the inferences? Are all the inferences fully warranted? Does the argument develop logically? Does it flow? Will readers find it interesting and significant?

Chapter 4 outlined the key components of historical narratives. Check your writing to make sure that your audience knows what they need to know in the correct order. Are terms, characters, and events introduced clearly? Are events presented in chronological sequence? If for some reason you have moved backwards in time—for instance to cover a different aspect of the same set of events—have you made the sequencing clear? Have you included all the relevant dates? Is there any extraneous information that does not belong in any of the main stories? Have you established a consistent voice as a narrator?

Evaluate Your Sentences and Word Choices

This book has already offered some advice on how to write sentences and how to choose the right words. While you are revising, you need to stand back and look at your sentences as your readers will. Have you chosen strong verbs? Is the order of ideas appropriate? Does every sentence follow logically from the one before it and develop a new idea?

Also look at your word choices as your audience will. Is your language free of jargon? Have you defined any specialized terms that readers may not be familiar with? Is there anything that readers are likely to find pretentious or unclear? Have you avoided contractions and colloquialisms?

> **TIP!** Do you find that you use the same words or phrases too often? If so, consult a thesaurus (easily available online and included in your word-processing program) to find alternatives.

Proofread the Final Draft

Proofreading is an essential part of writing history. If your writing is sprinkled with mistakes, no matter how minor, even your most brilliant work will look like a comedy of errors.

Proofreading takes time and patience. Chances are that by the time you start, you will already know parts of the paper so well that your eyes and mind will start to wander. Be disciplined. It's easier to spot mistakes on paper than on screen, so print out a copy and force yourself to read every word. When this gets too boring, put the paper aside for a short time and come back to it later. You might even try reading the pages in reverse order, so that you focus on the words rather than the argument and narrative. There is no way to make proofreading interesting, but it has to be done.

Proofread for Punctuation

When their work is criticized specifically for poor punctuation, history students sometimes complain to their professors that "This is not an English course!" True enough. However, history is mostly a written discipline, and those who can't communicate in writing will not succeed. Proper punctuation is not a frill: it is an absolute necessity. Look at the following two sentences quoted in a recent bestseller:

> A woman, without her man, is nothing.
> A woman: without her, man is nothing.[68]

Changing the punctuation changes the meaning entirely. It's said that during a heated debate in Britain's House of Lords, one member insulted another. The insulted lord demanded an apology and the offending lord replied: "I called the Right Honourable Lord a liar it is true and I am sorry for it. And the Right Honourable Lord may punctuate as he pleases."[69] Was he sorry to have said it? Was he sorry that the Lord was a liar? Punctuation would tell the tale.

Misunderstandings caused by imprecise punctuation are probably more common than you think. If you have trouble with punctuation, refer to Turabian or *The Chicago Manual of Style* for guidance. Many other writing manuals discuss punctuation as well.

Proofread for Spelling

Spelling errors can be the most embarrassing of all mistakes. (Or was that embarassing? Are you sure?) For that reason it's essential to use the spell-checking feature on your word-processing program. Just remember that spell-checkers don't think and are incapable of catching all spelling mistakes. In particular, they are not designed to catch mistakes involving homophones: words that sound the same but mean different things, such as "thrown" versus "throne," or "reign" versus "rein" versus "rain." As long as a word exists in the spell-checker's dictionary, it will not be recognized as an error, even if it makes no sense at all in the context of your paper. After running the spell-checker, therefore, you need to print out a hard copy and recheck it yourself.

Check for Consistent Spelling

British English is derived mainly from Latin, Germanic, and Norman French roots, and the spelling was standardized after 1755, when Samuel Johnson published his great dictionary. In 1828, Noah Webster published the first American English dictionary, in which he simplified the spellings of words he thought needlessly complicated. This explains the difference between American and British English spellings. While some historians don't care much which style their students use, and it must be acknowledged that typical Canadian usage does draw from both traditions, many historians in Canada prefer British English to American spelling. Whatever the style, it's important to be consistent. The best way to avoid mixing styles is to choose one dictionary, for instance *The Canadian Oxford Dictionary*, which is widely available, and follow its spellings. Internet sites that give comprehensive lists of American versus Canadian British spellings are also easy to find. If in doubt about which style to use for a particular course, ask your instructor.

Many of the differences between Canadian and American English spelling come at the ends of the words, so here is a short list of some of the most common:

Canadian	American	Example
-our	-or	harbour, colour
-re	-er	centre, theatre
-ce	-se	defence, offence
-ogue	-og	catalogue

Double-Check Possessives

Chances are that if you are learning to write history, you have already learned how to write a grammatical sentence. Even so, there is a type of grammatical error that is embarrassingly common even among professional historians. It involves the formation of the possessive, and most of the confusion surrounds words that end in the letter "s."

1. *Form the possessive of a singular noun by adding "'s."* This rule holds even when the word ends in the letter "s," as in "Cecil Rhodes's diamond mines," or "the duchess's letters."

   There are some minor exceptions to this rule. Traditionally, ancient names ending in "s" have taken only an apostrophe, as in "Moses' laws," "Jesus' name," or "Herodotus' histories." Since these constructions are somewhat awkward, however, many writers prefer to use "of" to form the possessive in such cases: "the laws of Moses," for instance, or "the name of Jesus." Notice also that the words "its" and "whose" are already possessive and do not take an apostrophe.

2. *Form the possessive of a plural noun by adding an apostrophe.* This is true when the plural is formed by adding an "s," for example, "the Redcoats' muskets" or "the Wright brothers' airplane."

3. *Don't use an apostrophe with initialisms or numbers.* It used to be standard practice to use an apostrophe to form the plural of initialisms (terms such as MP, CEO, or PC) and numbers: for example, "PC's were first manufactured during the 1980's." Most style manuals now recommend omitting the apostrophe in such cases: "PCs," "1980s." Use an apostrophe

only when there is the possibility of confusion, as in "There are two o's and two p's in apostrophe."

4. *Never use an apostrophe to form a plural.* Columbus did not discover "the America's." He discovered "the Americas" (at least some people think he did). Apostrophes do not denote the plural.

Check Your Formatting

Professors sometimes have their own preferences regarding formatting and paper presentation. Pay careful attention to any instructions you are given. If you have not received any specific directions, make sure that you have used a consistent word-processing format throughout the paper. A consistent format is crucial because aberrations are distracting. Your readers will also expect a simple format. Typically, history professors prefer a 12-point plain font with one-inch margins and lines double-spaced. Be sure that the pages are numbered, and that your name and the paper's title are on the first page. Modern printers can now often use both sides of the sheet, but your professor may prefer that you use one side only. Be sure to ask if it is not already specified. Some professors may also ask for a title page. This should include your name, the professor's name, the course name or number, and the date of submission, as well as the paper's title. While you are checking the format of the hard copy, be sure to check the elements that do not necessarily appear clearly on screen when you are writing, such as footnotes, margins, and page numbers.

> **TIP!** Now is a great time to very carefully reread the instructions for your assignment. Have you included every element the professor required?

Read Your Paper Aloud

Reading aloud is the oldest trick in the book for catching writing problems because it forces you to review every word. It should be the last thing you do before you submit your work. You may be surprised to find that you will hear mistakes that you did not see on the printed page. Your roommate may think you're eccentric, but your readers will appreciate the end result: a better piece of writing.

Submit Your Paper

Before submitting your paper, take one last look through to be sure everything is there, in the correct order and the right way up. Fasten the pages securely according to your professor's instructions. Be sure to make a copy of the finished product. Professors rarely misplace papers, but it can happen, and your life will be considerably easier if you have a replacement copy on hand. Be sure to keep absolutely all of your notes, drafts, and any other in-process materials in case your professor asks to see them. Then submit your paper with pride, knowing that you have done your best.

REVIEW

1. Take a break to give yourself some perspective.
2. Choose a meaningful title.
3. Ask someone else to read your paper and comment on it.
4. Revise, revise, revise—everything from arguments to spelling and punctuation.
5. Check and re-check.
6. Keep all notes and drafts.
7. Make a copy and save it!

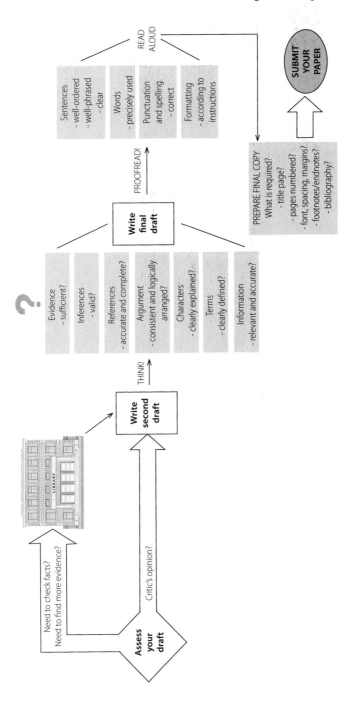

READ ALOUD

Sentences
- well-ordered
- well-phrased
- clear

Words
- precisely used

Punctuation and spelling
- correct

Formatting
- according to instructions

PROOFREAD!

Write final draft

Evidence
- sufficient?

Inferences
- valid?

References
- accurate and complete?

Argument
- consistent and logically arranged?

Characters
- clearly explained?

Terms
- clearly defined?

Information
- relevant and accurate?

THINK!

Write second draft

LIBRARY

PREPARE FINAL COPY
What is required?
- title page?
- pages numbered?
- font, spacing, margins?
- footnotes/endnotes?
- bibliography?

SUBMIT YOUR PAPER

Need to check facts?
Need to find more evidence?

Critic's opinion?

Assess your draft

Appendix A

Essay Concept Maps

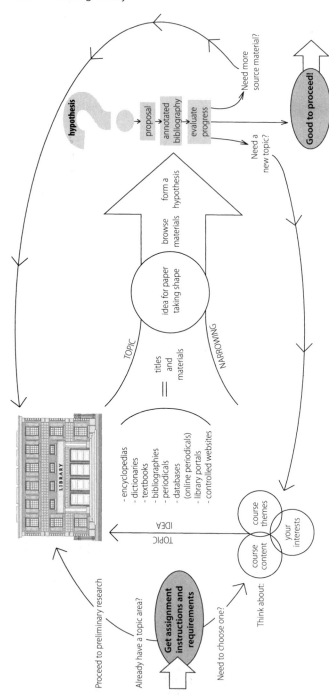

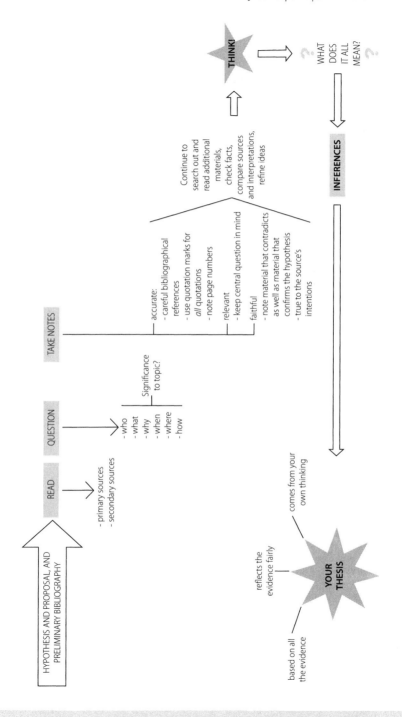

HYPOTHESIS AND PROPOSAL, AND PRELIMINARY BIBLIOGRAPHY

READ
- primary sources
- secondary sources

QUESTION
- who
- what
- why
- when
- where
- how

Significance to topic?

TAKE NOTES

accurate:
- careful bibliographical references
- use quotation marks for *all* quotations
- note page numbers

relevant
- keep central question in mind

faithful
- note material that contradicts as well as material that confirms the hypothesis
- true to the source's intentions

Continue to search out and read additional materials, check facts, compare sources and interpretations, refine ideas

THINK!

WHAT DOES IT ALL MEAN?

INFERENCES

YOUR THESIS

comes from your own thinking

reflects the evidence fairly

based on all the evidence

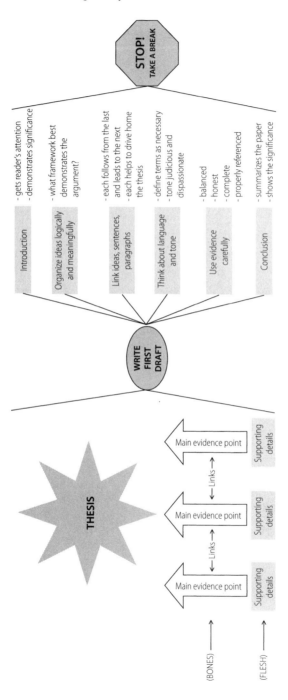

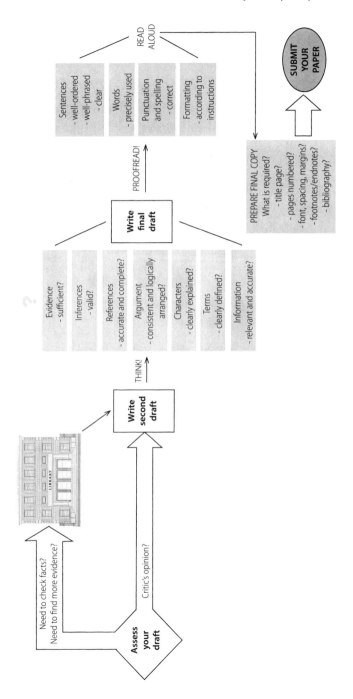

Appendix B

Citation Guide

As is explained in Chapter 5, virtually all history assignments require you to reference your sources, often by using footnotes or endnotes followed by a bibliography. The only difference between footnotes and endnotes is their placement: footnotes go at the bottom of the page and endnotes at the end of the paper. Otherwise they are identical. Their purpose is to tell readers exactly where you found your material. They should include all the information necessary for readers to look up your sources themselves and evaluate your use of them.

The notes refer to the specific points in your text where you have used material borrowed from others. These might typically be quotations, paraphrases, summaries, statistics, arguments, or interpretations. Notes usually include all publication information right down to the specific pages from which you took your information. Your bibliography, on the other hand, is an overall list of your sources; the list is arranged alphabetically by last name of author.

This section includes detailed information on how to format note and bibliography entries followed by a series of examples of the most commonly used types of sources. All entries conform to those in the sixteenth edition of *The Chicago Manual of Style*.

Footnotes and Endnotes

Every time you quote, paraphrase, summarize, or otherwise refer to someone else's material or ideas, create a note with a **superscript number** in the text. Start with number 1 at the beginning of the paper and keep going: don't start again with number 1 at the top of each page (or the beginning of each new section), and don't use the same number every time you refer to the same source. Each superscript number refers your reader to an accompanying reference note either at the bottom of the page (a footnote) or on a separate page at the end of the paper (an endnote).

When you read, you will find that note references are usually placed at the end of the sentence: "J.R. Miller argues that the First Nations peoples in Canada consistently sought to determine their own paths."[4] The number belongs at the end of the sentence, rather than following Miller's name, because the entire sentence concerns his book *Skyscrapers Hide the Heavens,* 3rd ed. (Toronto: University of Toronto Press, 2000). The most usual time when it might be appropriate to place the note in the middle of a sentence would be if the latter part of the sentence referred to a second author and it was necessary to distinguish the two. If no confusion would exist, there is no problem putting multiple sources into one note; just enter them in the same order in which you used them in the sentence and separate them from each other with semi-colons.

It is also possible to use what is sometimes called a "blanket note." This is useful particularly when you need to write something reasonably non-specific and non-argumentative. For example, if you were writing a biography of Louis Riel and you wanted to start with a paragraph outlining the major events of his life, you might well pull this together using material from several sources. In this case your note number would be placed at the end of either the first or last sentence in the paragraph. The note itself could read something like this: "For all chronological material in this paragraph, see the following sources:..." Then you would list the works you had used, together with the relevant page numbers. Of course, if you had included specific quotations, or paraphrases, or something controversial in the paragraph, these would need their own references.

Note that although history professors may prefer your notes to list the complete publishing information the first time you refer to a given work, it is not technically necessary to do so—all this information must be included in your bibliography anyway. Be sure to check for your professor's preferences. In any case, a second or subsequent reference to the same source can be shortened.

Formatting Footnotes and Endnotes

Most word-processing programs today now handle references automatically: all you have to do is select the appropriate format (footnote or endnote; number style) and specify where each note should be inserted. All notes contain essentially the same information because they are designed for the same purpose: they direct your readers to the sources on which you have relied. Thus they include information like author, title, place of publication, publisher, date of publication and the relevant page or pages. Notes should be single-spaced in the same font size as the main text, and each note is generally formatted as a single sentence, punctuated with commas and colons. The first line of the note begins with an indentation from the left margin. After the note number, insert a period and a space.

Here is the general pattern for a very basic note:

#. Author's name, *Title* (Place of publication: publisher, date of publication), page.

Example:

7. Sarah Smith, *The Plight of the Purple Orangutan* (Timbucktoo: Superstar University Press, 2009), 47.

Note that while the book title here is italicized, it is also perfectly acceptable to underline book titles—choose one style and stick with it. Article titles, by the way, are placed into quotation marks.

Use a shortened version when you refer again to a source that you have already used at least once before. A shortened version of this note would look like this:

7. Smith, *Plight*, 47.

Bibliographies

As mentioned above, the bibliography is the list of all sources consulted in the preparation of a paper. It is arranged alphabetically according to authors' last names, although for historical sources this can sometimes be difficult to figure out. (See pages 159–161 for examples.) Include in your bibliography all the sources you consulted meaningfully in the preparation of your assignment, whether or not you specifically quoted or otherwise borrowed from them. If you read them and they made any real difference to your thinking, then include them. The bibliography is always placed at the end of the paper.

Formatting Bibliographies

Again, many word-processing programs will create bibliographies automatically, as will referencing programs such as Zotero or Citavi. You simply need to select the style you prefer. For history, usually it would be Chicago style. Bibliographies are designed to allow your readers a swift look at all of your sources and, with three main differences, they include all of the same information that went into the notes. One difference is that works not included in the notes because you did not use them very specifically will still appear in the bibliography. A second difference is that the first line of each entry is placed at the left-hand margin while second and subsequent lines are indented. This allows the authors' last names to stand out clearly. The third difference lies in the punctuation: each portion of the bibliographical reference is set off by a period, so the reference is punctuated as if it is a series of tiny sentences.

Here is the general pattern for the bibliographical entry to go with the note above:

Author's name. *Title*. Place of publication: publisher, date of publication.

Example:

Smith, Sarah. *The Plight of the Orangutan*. Timbucktoo: Superstar University Press, 2009.

Note that no page numbers are included here: the entire book is being listed.

Citation Examples: Notes

Use the examples below as models for how to reference the types of work you may quite commonly come across. If you do not find what you need here, consult Turabian's *Student Guide* or *The Chicago Manual*, both of which have many more examples.

A book with a single author
Endnotes and footnotes to books should be written like this:

11. John Mack Farragher, *A Great and Noble Scheme: The Tragic Story of the Expulsion of the Acadians from Their American Homeland* (New York: Norton, 2005), 35–39.

The author's first name comes first, information about the publisher is placed in parentheses, and a comma precedes the page numbers. There is usually no need for a "p." or "pp." in front of the page numbers, unless there is some risk of confusion with other numbers in the citation.

A book with multiple authors

11. Sally Ross and Alphonse Deveau, *The Acadians of Nova Scotia Past and Present* (Halifax: Nimbus, 1992), 73.

Note that in this example Ross is listed before Deveau. List the authors in the order that the book lists them on the title page; do not rearrange them alphabetically. If the book has more than four authors, include only the first one in the note, followed by *et al.*, which is short for *et alia* or "and others." In the bibliography you must list all of the authors.

A multi-volume book

12. J. Murray Beck, *Joseph Howe*, 2 vols. (Kingston and Montreal: McGill-Queen's University Press, 1982), 2: 133.

An edited book

13. Allan Greer, ed., *The Jesuit Relations: Natives and Missionaries in Seventeenth-Century North America* (Boston: Bedford/St. Martins, 2000), 47–53.

A revised edition

14. Alan D. McMillan, *Native Peoples and Culture of Canada: An Anthropological Overview,* 2nd ed. (Vancouver and Toronto: Douglas & McIntyre, 1995), 113.

A chapter in an edited book

15. Peter H. Harrison, "Life in a Logging Camp," in *Home Truths: Highlights from B.C. History*, ed. Richard Mackie and Graeme Wynn (Madeira Park, BC: Harbour, 2012), 340.

A document in an anthology

16. J.B. Jukes, "Sealing off Newfoundland," in *First Drafts: Eyewitness Accounts from Canada's Past*, ed. J.L. Granatstein and Norman Hilmer (Toronto: Thomas Allen & Son, 2002), 64.

An anonymous work

17. *A shorte and plaine Table orderly disposing the Principles of religion, and first of the first Table of the Law, whereby we may examine our selves*. (London, 1580).

Citing Scholarly Articles

Scholarly articles by historians are usually published in either scholarly journals or edited collections. Note that article titles are placed in quotation marks.

An article in an edited collection

Notice that the format for an article in an edited collection resembles a book citation.

37. Kelly Olson, "The Appearance of the Young Roman Girl," in *Roman Dress and the Fabric of Roman Culture*, eds. J. Edmonson and A. Keith (Toronto: University of Toronto Press, 2008), 143–44.

An article in a journal

Journal articles are cited somewhat differently. The author and title are given first, followed by the title of the journal (treated as if it is a book title), its volume and number, the date in parentheses, and a colon followed by the page number. Here is a simple citation, followed by one that is more complex.

> 38. Fanny Dolansky, "Playing Gender: Girls, Dolls, and Adult Ideals in the Roman World," *Classical Antiquity* 31 no. 2 (2012): 264.
>
> 39. Sarah Levin-Richardson, "'*Fututa Sum Hic*': Female Subjectivity and Agency in Pompeian Sexual Graffiti," *Classical Journal* 108 (February/March 2013): 327.

Ordinarily, an article title is simply placed in quotation marks, followed by the italicized (or underlined) journal or book title and the publication information. The second example above includes a title that is in part a quotation, so it needs an extra set of quotation marks. Because the quotation is in a foreign language, it is italicized.

Citing Works of Journalism

An article in a magazine
Citations of articles in magazines should provide the name of the author (if it is listed), article title, name of the magazine, date, section (if the article is part of a regular feature), and page number. If the author's name is not listed, start the entry with the article title.

> 50. Charlie Gillis and Chris Sorensen, "Finding Franklin," *Maclean's*, September 22, 2014, 42.

An article in a newspaper
Newspapers get similar treatment, except that since they are often published in multiple editions, not all of which are the same, no page number is needed.

> 51. Paul Watson, "Former Trawler Helped Land Big One," *Toronto Star*, September 17, 2014.

Unpublished Secondary Works

Sometimes, in the course of your research, you may come across an unpublished secondary work, such as a thesis or dissertation that could be a useful source. If you do, ask your librarian if you need the author's permission to read or cite it. Theses and dissertations are cited as follows:

> 8. Nanci Delayen, "The Fabian Society and Eugenics, 1885–1914" (master's thesis, University of Saskatchewan, 1998), 57.

Interviews, Lectures, and Oral Presentations

These kinds of citations should give the name of the source and the place and date on which he or she gave you the information. Courtesy dictates that private conversations should not be cited unless you have the permission of the person you interviewed. See the section on "oral history projects" in Chapter 1 for more information on oral history.

> 76. Ernest Hemingway, interview with the author, Key West, Florida, September 6, 1932.

Citing Archival Sources

Every archive is organized differently, so the main rule for archival citations is to provide all the information necessary for a reader to trace your source. Fortunately, some institutions provide researchers with guidelines for citing material from their collections. Among them is Britain's National Archives, which in 2003 took over what was formerly known as the Public Records Office (PRO). The following citation directs readers to the PRO section of the National Archives Colonial Office (CO) files, item number 167/661:

61. Lees to Knutsford, with minutes by Wingfield, 9 Jan. 1891, National Archives: PRO CO 167/661.

If you are conducting research in an archive, be sure to ask if there is a correct way to cite their sources. Also be sure to spell out any abbreviations the first time you use them, so that your readers will know what they mean.

Citing Internet Sources

References to web sources follow the same principles as any other citation: they should give readers all the information they need to find those sources themselves. Thus Internet citations should give the full Uniform Resource Locator (URL) address of the page where the material was found, not just the relevant home page.

At the same time it is important to acknowledge that, whereas print sources are more or less permanent and can almost always be located in a major research library, Internet sources can change or disappear at any time. Therefore it is essential to record the date when you accessed the material, along with the date of publication if it is available. It's also advisable to keep a printout of every web page you cite from the day when you used it; that way, if a reader challenges your use of the material, you will have the evidence even if the page has changed or disappeared.

Of course, your citation should also include the author, title, and whatever additional information is available. Thus to cite an article from an online version of a print journal, you would begin in exactly the same way you would for a conventional print article, listing the author, title, journal, issue number, and date. Then list the date of access, followed by a comma, and finally the URL.

Now suppose you wanted to cite some archival material—specifically, an article that appeared in the (Victoria) *British Colonist* in 1869—that you found on the website called *Who Killed William Robinson?* Created by Ruth Sandwell and John Lutz, this site is now part of the "Great Unsolved Mysteries in Canadian History Project." For each mystery, the site reproduces many primary and secondary sources, including newspaper articles, photographs, legal documents, correspondence, diaries, artists' reconstructions, paintings, and historians' commentaries. Use the following method to cite an archival newspaper article from the Robinson site:

> 42. "Threats," *British Colonist*, June 3, 1869. *Who Killed William Robinson?* (website), Ruth Sandwell and John Lutz, accessed 17 August 2010, http://www.canadianmysteries.ca/sites/robinson/home/indexen.html.

If you know the newspaper page and column number, include it after the publication date. Note that in some cases a website will provide only one main address, as shown on its home pages. Some sites show individual addresses for each section or document, so be sure to check carefully for these and to include them where appropriate.

Citing Books and Articles Accessed Online

Again, follow the same principles as for all other citations: give your readers the information that allows them to find the materials for themselves. Thus you must include all of the usual information such as author, title and publication details, but also Internet identifiers. These might be uniform resource locators (URLs) or digital object identifiers (DOIs.)

The URL, which usually begins with something like "http://www." is present for all Internet resources, and it will lead a reader directly to a source. This is often an easy resource identifier, but it is important to realize that URLs can move, change, or even disappear entirely. The DOI is a long series of numbers. The first few designate a DOI registration agency. These are followed by a forward slash, and then a series of digits that come from the publisher. If it is present, the DOI is a better resource identifier because it is designed to be permanent and unique for a specific resource. Sometimes the DOI follows the URL.

How does this all work in practice?

The DOI for Jo Fox's article "Propaganda and the Flight of Rudolf Hess, 1941–45," which appeared in the *Journal of Modern History* in March 2011, is 10.1086/658050. To cite this article in your paper, you normally would give all of the usual publication information, followed by the URL, which is http://www.jstor.org/stable/10.1086/658050. Your readers could then do a simple Internet search for the DOI, which would lead them to the article. *The Chicago Manual of Style* suggests that you need not include the full URL if a DOI is available, but you may wish to ask your professor if this is acceptable.

One other detail is worth emphasizing: when you reference an online source, it is customary to include your date of access. Enter this date immediately before the URL.

Here are some common examples:

Books accessed online

43. Peter Pigott, *Air Canada: The History*. n.p.: Toronto: Dundurn [2014], 2014. Capilano University Library Catalogue, EBSCOhost (accessed December 22, 2014), Chapter 3.

The n.p. above refers to the fact that the electronic version of this book has no page numbers listed. In such a case, try to help out your readers by listing the chapter or section to which you have referred. 2014 is listed twice to specify that the book was published in two versions, hard copy and electronic, both in 2014.

Articles accessed online

44. Alexander W.G. Herd, "A 'Common Appreciation': Eisenhower, Canada, and Continental Air Defense, 1953–1954," *Journal of Cold War Studies*, 13, no. 3 (2011): 4, ProjectMUSE (accessed December 15, 2014).

If your article lists a DOI, then include it at the end of your citation.

How to Repeat a Citation

In the past, most writers used Latin abbreviations such as "ibid." ("the same"), "loc. cit." ("in the place cited"), and "op. cit." ("in the work cited") to indicate repeated references to the same source. Today, some writers still use "ibid." when two consecutive notes cite exactly the same source, right down to the page number, but most prefer a simpler system. The first time you cite a source, give the full citation; then for subsequent references give only the author's last name, a short version of the title, and the page number(s). Here are some examples from Canadian historians writing about the First World War:

> 11. Margaret MacMillan, *The War that Ended Peace: The Road to 1914* (Toronto: Allen Lane, 2013), 191.
>
> 12. MacMillan, *War*, 45.
>
> 13. André Gerolymatos, *The Balkan Wars: Myth, Reality, and the Eternal Conflict* (Toronto: Stoddart Publishing, 2001), 42–44.
>
> 14. Gerolymatos, *Balkan Wars*, 48.
>
> 15. MacMillan, *War*, 544.
>
> 16. Ibid.
>
> 17. Margaret MacMillan, *Paris 1919: Six Months That Changed the World* (New York: Random House, 2001), 124.
>
> 18. Gerolymatos, *Balkan Wars*, 545–52.
>
> 19. MacMillan, *Paris*, 137.

If you decide to use "ibid.," be extra careful at the revision stage: it's easy to separate consecutive entries when you are moving material around. Note also that you may be working with multiple sources from the same author or sources that have similar titles, so you'll need to be careful to shorten them in ways that differentiate them from each other.

Citing a Quotation of a Quotation

Historians prefer to quote from original sources. If you see a primary source quotation in a secondary work and you want to quote it as well, you are expected to check the primary source and assess the accuracy of the quotation yourself.

Sometimes, though, you may not have access to the original source. Suppose you have read about the treatment of French prisoners of war in Dennis Smith's book *The Prisoners of Cabrera: Napoleon's Forgotten Soldiers 1809–1814*. Smith quotes from an 1813 article in the newspaper *El Nueva Diario del Liberal Napoléon*:

> Humanity cries out and the heart trembles to see three thousand or more men abandoned on an uninhabited desert island, exposed to storms, naked and hungry when weather blocks the supply ships. If they were cruel and armed enemies, we would not treat them with such atrocious torments. . . .

Now you want to use this colourful passage in your own work, but have not been able to track down a copy of the original work. You can still use the quotation if you attribute it as follows:

> 27. R.A., as cited in Denis Smith, *The Prisoners of Cabrera: Napoeon's Forgotten Soldiers 1809–1814* (Toronto: MacFarlane, Walter and Ross, 2001), 157.

Note that the author, whose full name is not known, is correctly listed as R.A., even though you read the passage in a book by Smith. Since the source is not well-known, it would be an excellent idea to mention in your own text that this quotation comes from a contemporary newspaper.

Discursive Notes

In the course of your reading, you may notice that some authors use endnotes or footnotes not only to cite their sources but to address points of interpretation, or even to digress from their subjects. These **discursive notes** can be useful to the author, but readers often find them annoying. If something is important enough to say, why not say it in the main body of the text? Think carefully before introducing a discursive note: don't use it as a way to sneak additional material into the paper without exceeding your page limit.

Know the Difference between Notes and Bibliographies

Unless your paper is very short, or based on only one source, it will usually require a bibliography: an alphabetical list of all the sources you consulted in preparing it, regardless of whether you actually used them directly for things like quotations or summaries. Notes, on the other hand, refer your readers to the specific sources from which you borrowed material. Bibliography entries are in some ways similar in form to notes. However, the main elements of each entry are separated with periods rather than commas and parentheses, and the author's name is reversed, last name first (if there is more than one author, the others' names are not reversed). For an article, inclusive page numbers should follow the issue number. Bibliographies also usually have a hanging indent, meaning that the first line of an entry is five spaces to the left of the following lines:

Daschuk, James. *Clearing the Plains: Disease, Politics of Starvation and the Loss of Aboriginal Life*. Regina: University of Regina Press, 2013.

Hogue, Michael. "Disputing the Medicine Line: The Plains Cree and the Canadian-American Border, 1876–85." In *One West, Two Myths*, edited by Carol Higham and Robert Thacker, 85–108. Calgary: University of Calgary Press, 2004.

Vance, Jonathan F. *A History of Canadian Culture*. Toronto: Oxford University Press, 2009.

Vogt, David and David Alexander Gamble. "'You Don't Suppose the Dominion Government Wants to Cheat the Indians?': The Grand Trunk Pacific Railway and the Fort George Reserve." *BC Studies* 166 (Summer 2010): 55–72.

For other questions about notes and bibliographies, consult either Turabian or *The Chicago Manual of Style*, both of which offer much more comprehensive listings. They also cover the in-text author–date citation systems that are more commonly used in literature and the social sciences, notably the Modern Language Association (MLA) style and the American Psychological Association (APA) style. Note that the recent seventh edition of the *MLA Handbook* includes a section on endnotes and footnotes. Earlier editions cover this information in an appendix.

Appendix C

Suggested History Resources

It would be impossible to list all of the thousands of websites that could be of interest to history students, so this is just a tiny representative sample designed to give you an idea of what you might find if you "let your fingers [and your imagination] do the walking."

As a general rule, do think about looking on the websites of museums, art galleries, libraries both public and academic, archives public and private, universities in general and history departments in particular. Also, look for sites run by governments, from federal to municipal. Finally, remember that many encyclopedias, atlases, dictionaries, and other reference works can be accessed online.

Please note that the lists below do not include sites that include a lot of third-party advertising or other commercial material. In general, be cautious of sites that do.

Writing and Citations

www.chicagomanualofstyle.org
This is the online version of *The Chicago Manual of Style*, the best source for how to reference in history papers. It includes a Chicago Style Quick Citation Guide that is most useful.

www.press.uchicago.edu/books/turabian/turabian_citation guide.html
Turabian online also has a useful citation guide. Just click on the notes and bibliography tab on the front page and many examples of correct referencing appear.

General and World History

Note that a few of the sites listed here also refer to Canadian history.

www.fordham.edu/halsall
This is the Fordham University gateway to an astonishingly rich set of collections of primary documents. They are arranged into separate "history sourcebooks" on topics such as ancient, modern,

Islamic, women, African, gay and lesbian—you name it. You are likely to find a sourcebook of primary documents and other resources here.

www.gutenberg.org
The Project Gutenberg gateway gives you access to tens of thousands of free e-books, both fiction and non-fiction, that you can download or read online. For history, click on the "book categories" tab on the left, and then on "history bookshelf." You also might want to check the "Social Sciences bookshelf."

www.besthistorysites.net/indexphp/general-resources
This American site offers links to a host of resources. Many are American, but sites particularly from Britain are also included. Thus you can link to PBS, BBC, History Teacher, virtual libraries, and so on. A lot of the sites are designed for teachers at all grade levels, so there are lesson plans and plenty of suggested activities such as quizzes and crossword puzzles as well as links to historical resources themselves. A good site to explore.

www.historyonthenet.com
History on the Net includes resources carefully arranged into specific categories such as Mayans, Aztecs, Vikings, world wars, and a host of others.

www.eh-resources.org/links/index.html
The site for Environmental History on the Web provides links to resources worldwide. The homepage also incudes a useful link to the Integrated Database in Canadian Environmental History.

www.library.utm.utoronto.ca
The main page for the University of Toronto's library includes a section labelled "Starting Points." Click on "history" and look in the "selected links and websites" section to find links for "general," North American, European and Asian history—one big category under the North American heading, of course, is Canada.

labyrinth.georgetown.edu
This site, maintained by Georgetown University, serves as a gateway for medieval studies. The homepage says that it provides links to "databases, services, texts, and images around the world" under a host of categories such as architecture, chivalry, church history, manuscripts, philosophy, and women. You can also search this site by keyword.

archive.is/eawc.evansville.edu
Evansville University maintains the "Exploring Ancient World Cultures" site, which provides both primary sources and essays on a host of world history topics both ancient and medieval. The site also has chronologies, images, and Web links.

www.ipl.org
The Internet Public Library is maintained mostly by volunteers from Drexel University in Philadelphia. It allows you to search for resources under a variety of categories. Find history materials under "Arts and Humanities." Here you can find links to public libraries all over North America, a link to the Canadian literature archive, and one entitled "Historical Research in Europe: A Guide to Archives and Libraries." Another very useful link on the homepage takes you to newspapers and magazines from all over the world.

(Mostly) Canadian History

Note that Chapter 2 includes references to many Canadian history sites—these are not reproduced in this list.

www.virtualmuseum.ca
Canada's Virtual Museum site gives easy links to several thousand quite varied heritage institutions and virtual exhibits. Check this site for everything from the County Museum of Yarmouth, Nova Scotia, through the Sudbury Region Police Museum, to Vancouver's Holocaust Education Centre. This site also has a link to the Canadian Heritage Information Network.

www.historymuseum.ca
This is the website for the Canadian Museum of History, located in Gatineau, Quebec. Most useful for the history student is the collection of Canadian historical photographs. This site also links to the very interesting Virtual Museum of New France.

www.activehistory.ca
This is the website for the Canadian arm of a much wider Active History movement devoted to presenting the work of historians to the public. The point is to show the importance of the past to the present. The website has academic papers, exhibits, and so on, and can connect you to a host of activities.

shcyhome.org
The website for the Society for the History of Children and Youth is largely, but not solely, concerned with Canadian history. The website includes a number of course syllabi, many of which include bibliographical lists.

www.graphichistorycollective.com
This site is run from Simon Fraser University in Vancouver, and is devoted to exploration of comics and politically radical history.

www.saskarchives.com
Saskatchewan has a very active archival program, and this fascinating website connects you to a host of materials. It includes everything from court, government, and land documents, through photographs, diagrams, maps, and moving images, to family history research materials and even materials from private collections. The City of Regina Virtual Archive, linked to the Saskatchewan archive project, contains thousands of documents and images.

Note that other Canadian cities also have online archives that are worth looking at.

www.peel.library.ualberta.ca
Peel's Prairie Provinces, a website maintained by the University of

Alberta, contains books, newspapers, postcards, maps, and an online bibliography.

www.mun.ca/mha
The Maritime History Archive at the Memorial University of Newfoundland is a collection of documents relating to maritime history in the North Atlantic world. You can look for ships, crew lists, statistics, and so on.

www.canadianmysteries.ca
This is the home of Great Unsolved Mysteries in Canadian History, a fascinating site that features documents, maps, photographs, and diagrams focused on a number of unsolved mysteries.

Glossary

The numbers in parentheses refer to the pages where the terms appear bold. All terms are defined here as they are used in this book.

analytical essay (70): An essay that examines an analytical problem (e.g., the relationship between science and culture). An analytical essay uses short narratives to shed light on the concept or problem under examination.

annotated bibliography (42): A list of sources that includes not only the publishing information but also a brief description of each work.

archival material (42): Historical material, typically artifacts and primary documents, stored in archives.

argument (1): In a court case, the lawyers for each side argue their case—that is, they present their interpretation of the evidence—in such a way as to persuade their audience (the judge and jury). Like lawyers, historians frequently dispute one another's arguments as a way to explore knowledge and spark ideas.

bibliography (17): A list of the books, articles, and other documents on which an author has relied. All the relevant publishing information, including author (and/or editor), title, place and date of publication, and publisher, must be included.

block quotation (80): A quotation that is longer than three lines, set off from the main text in its own indented block, without quotation marks.

catalogue (21): When used in reference to a library, this refers to the list of the library's holdings. This list is usually accessed online and can usually be searched by author, title, or keywords.

citation system (89): The particular system used to cite sources in a given work. Historians typically use the Chicago or Turabian system, based on footnotes (or endnotes) and bibliographies. Other citation systems include MLA and APA, both of which use parenthetical referencing within the text.

citation (21): A reference note. Most citations include a specific page reference.

cliché (127): A trite, overused phrase; for example, "in the nick of time."

colloquial language (123): Informal or casual language, including slang and contractions like "it's" that are not appropriate for formal history papers.

database (27): An online collection of materials such as documents or journal articles that are useful in specific fields of study. Often available only through library subscription.

deduction (62): Deductive reasoning reaches reasonable conclusions based on sometimes limited evidence; the most likely explanation.

discursive note (168): A footnote or endnote that serves some purpose other than source identification (e.g., to clarify or expand on some aspect of the text). To be used sparingly, if at all.

draft (1): An early version of a piece of writing. For an essay, you should expect to write two or three drafts.

ellipses (81): Three dots (…) inserted into a quotation to show where words have been omitted.

endnote (89): See **footnote**.

euphemism (126): An evasive word or phrase used to soften the message or avoid giving offence; for example, "follically challenged" used in place of "bald."

footnote (35): A reference note (flagged by a superscript number in the text) that identifies the source(s) on which a particular passage is based. Footnotes appear at the bottom of the relevant text pages; endnotes appear on separate pages at the end of the text. Most word-processing programs will create either form automatically.

historiography (vii): The study of the writing of history; the study of the discipline itself.

hypothesis (41): The question or proposition that drives research on a specific topic.

induction (63): Inductive reasoning reaches generalized conclusions based on putting sometimes many pieces of evidence together.

inference (55): A conclusion based on the examination of evidence.

jargon (122): Technical or specialized words or phrases; generally inappropriate for use outside specific professions or groups.

narrative essay (72): An essay that may include analytical points but focuses on telling a single chronological story and generally arrives at one major conclusion.

paraphrase (78): A rewording of a source's statement in roughly the same number of words (a shorter rewording is a summary).

peer review (21): Pre-publication review of a book or article by one or more professionals in the field to assess its accuracy and credibility and make recommendations for revisions. Articles published in scholarly journals are generally peer-reviewed. Some journals call this "refereed."

plagiarism (78): The use of someone else's words or ideas without proper acknowledgement.

popular history (4): A book or article written for the general public rather than for a scholarly audience.

primary source (6): A source written or created in the time period under study; a first-hand account.

scholarly history (4): History written for a scholarly audience, particularly other historians. Scholarly history is usually based on original research and contributes new information or interpretations to the field. Such works have generally undergone rigorous peer review and editing.

secondary source (7): Typically, a

book or article based on primary sources. The works written by historians are generally secondary sources.

summary (78): A concise restatement of a source's discussion, argument, etc.

superscript number (156): A small number written or printed above the line of text and used for referencing purposes. Each number corresponds to a footnote or endnote in which the author lists all the relevant publication and other information as necessary. Most word-processing programs today have automatic footnote or endnote functions, usually accessed through "insert."

thesis (17): The central point that a piece of historical writing sets out to maintain or prove; usually introduced early in the work in a "thesis statement."

transition sentence (96): A sentence that connects one part of an argument with another; typically used to end one paragraph or begin the next.

Notes

1. Margaret MacMillan, *The Uses and Abuses of History* (Toronto: Viking Canada, 2008), xi.
2. Peter Novick, *That Noble Dream: The "Objectivity Question" and the American Historical Profession* (Cambridge: Cambridge University Press, 1988), 7.
3. Thucydides, *The Peloponnesian War*, trans. Rex Warner (New York: Penguin Books, 1954; repr. 1984), 145.
4. Ruth Sandwell, ed., *To the Past: History Education, Public Memory, and Citizenship in Canada* (Toronto: University of Toronto Press, 2006), 10.
5. Arthur J. Ray, *"I Have Lived Here Since the World Began": An Illustrated History of Canadian Native People*, 3rd ed. (Toronto: Key Porter, 2010).
6. Reinhold Kramer, *Mordecai Richler: Leaving St. Urbain* (Montreal and Kingston: McGill-Queen's University Press, 2008); Joe King, *From the Ghetto to the Main: The Story of Jews in Montreal* (Montreal: Montreal Jewish Publication Society, 2001).
7. John H. Arnold, *History: A Very Short Introduction* (Oxford: Oxford University Press, 2000), 13.
8. Trevor Smith, Capilano University Library, 12 September 2014, personal interview.
9. M. Brook Taylor and Doug Owram, eds., *Canadian History: A Reader's Guide*, 2 vols. (Toronto: University of Toronto Press, 1994); Norah Story, *The Oxford Companion to Canadian History and Literature* (Toronto: Oxford University Press, 1967); William Toye, ed., *Supplement to the Oxford Companion to Canadian History and Literature* (Toronto: Oxford University Press, 1973); Brian Gobbett and Robert , eds., *Introducing Canada: An Annotated Bibliography of Canadian History in English* (Lanham, MD:

Scarecrow Press, 1998); and Mary E. Bond, ed., *Canadian Reference Sources: An Annotated Bibliography* (Vancouver: University of British Columbia Press, 1996). *Canadian Reference Sources* also includes works in French.
10. *Bulletin of the Historical Association* (UK: Blackwell, for the Historical Association, 1997–present).
11. Diana Pedersen, *Changing Women, Changing History: A Bibliography of the History of Women in Canada* (Ottawa: Carleton University Press, 1996); George P. Murdock, *The Ethnographic Bibliography of North America*, 4th ed. (New Haven: Human Relations Area Files, 1975); *4th edition Supplement 1973-1987* (New Haven: Human Relations Area Files, 1990); Owen A. Cook, *The Canadian Military Experience 1867-1995: A Bibliography* (Ottawa: Department of National Defence, 1997); Barbara J. Lowther, *A Bibliography of British Columbia: Laying the Foundations, 1849-1899* (Victoria: University of Victoria, 1968); and Linda Hale, *The Vancouver Centennial Bibliography* (Vancouver: Vancouver Historical Society, 1986).
12. *The Canadian Encyclopedia* (Edmonton: Hurtig, 1985, 1988 and online at www.thecanadianencyclopedia.com) and *The Canadian Encyclopedia: Year 2000 Edition* (Toronto: McClelland & Stewart, 1999); *The Dictionary of Canadian Biography*, 15 vols. (Toronto: University of Toronto Press and Les Presses de l'Université Laval, 1966–2005). (Note that *The Dictionary of Canadian Biography* is also available online at www.biographi.ca/en/index.php). Gerald Hallowell, ed., *The Oxford Companion to Canadian History* (Toronto: Oxford University Press, 2004). The new *Oxford Companion* does not simply replace or update the older

version, which is now a bit elderly but still useful. The new *Companion* contains an encyclopedic series of short articles on a vast number of Canadian history topics. Paul Robert Magosci, ed., *The Encyclopedia of Canada's Peoples* (Toronto: University of Toronto Press, 1999). *Canadian Who's Who* (Toronto: University of Toronto Press) has been published annually since 1910. It can be found in microfiche for the years 1898–1975, on CD-ROM since 1997 and also online at www.canadianwhoswho.ca. *The Canadian Annual Review of Politics and Public Affairs* (Toronto: University of Toronto Press) contains synopses of each year's affairs. It is published several years after the fact, so that the volume published in 2006 covers up to 2000. Richard W. Pound, ed., *Fitzhenry and Whiteside Book of Canadian Facts and Dates*, 3rd ed. (Markham, ON: Fitzhenry and Whiteside, 2005) is a basic list of events and people from "the making of a planet" through 2003, and it also contains a bibliography section.

13. R. Cole Harris et al., eds., *The Historical Atlas of Canada*, 3 vols. (Toronto: University of Toronto Press, 1987–1993) and William G. Dean et al., eds., *The Concise Historical Atlas of Canada* (Toronto: University of Toronto Press, 1998).

14. Sean Kheraj, *Inventing Stanley Park: An Environmental History* (Vancouver: UBC Press, 2013).

15. H.V. Nelles, *A Little History of Canada* (Toronto: Oxford University Press, 2004).

16. Heather Robertson, *Measuring Mother Earth: How Joe the Kid Became Tyrell of the North* (Toronto: McClelland & Stewart, 2007).

17. For a broader discussion of these research questions, see Richard Marius and Melvin E. Page, *A Short Guide to Writing about History*, 6th ed. (New York: Pearson/Longman, 2007), 32–9.

18. Wendy Wickwire, "To See Ourselves as the Other's Other: Nlaka'pamux

Contact Narratives," *Canadian Historical Review* 75 no. 1 (1994): 1–20.

19. Loren R. Graham, *The Ghost of the Executed Engineer: Technology and the Fall of the Soviet Union* (Cambridge: Harvard University Press, 1993).

20. Hippocrates, *Precepts*, as quoted by Chester W. Starr in *A History of the Ancient World*, 3rd ed. (New York: Oxford University Press, 1983), 331.

21. Walt Whitman, "The Real War Will Never Get in the Books," in *Specimen Days* (New York: Signet Classic, 1961), 112.

22. Deborah E. Lipstadt, *Denying the Holocaust* (New York: Penguin, 1993).

23. Arnold, *History*, 13.

24. Cole Harris, *The Resettlement of British Columbia: Essays on Colonialism and Geographical Change* (Vancouver: University of British Columbia Press, 1997).

25. Prasenjit Duara, *Culture, Power, and the State: Rural North China, 1900–1942* (Stanford: Stanford University Press, 1988); Philip C.C. Huang, *The Peasant Economy and Social Change in North China* (Stanford: Stanford University Press, 1985); Ramon Myers, *The Chinese Peasant Economy: Agricultural Development in Hopei and Shantung, 1840–1940* (Cambridge: Harvard University Press, 1970).

26. Gerald L. Geison, *The Private Science of Louis Pasteur* (Princeton: Princeton University Press, 1995), 149–56.

27. John Ashdown-Hill, *The Last Days of Richard III and the Fate of his DNA* (Stroud, Gloucerstershire: The History Press, 2013); Philippa Langley and Michael Jones, *The King's Grave: the Discovery of Richard III's Lost Burial Place and the Clues it Holds* (New York: St. Martin's Press, 2013).

28. Robin Fisher, *Contact and Conflict: Indian–European Relations in British Columbia, 1774–1890* (Vancouver: University of British Columbia Press, 1977; 2nd ed. 1992).

29. Jules David Prown, "Mind in Matter:

An Introduction to Material Culture Theory and Method," in *Material Life in America, 1600–1860*, ed. Robert Blair St. George (Boston: Northeastern University Press, 1991), 17–35. Thanks to Elizabeth Abrams for suggesting this article.

30. Charles S. Maier, *The Unmasterable Past: History, Holocaust, and German National Identity* (Cambridge: Harvard University Press, 1988), 1.

31. John Mack Farragher, *A Great and Noble Scheme: The Tragic Story of the Expulsion of the French Acadians from Their American Homeland* (New York: Norton, 2005), 473.

32. Georges Lefebvre, *The Coming of the French Revolution*, trans. R.R. Palmer (Princeton: Princeton University Press, 1947; rev. ed. 1989).

33. Betty Jo Teeter Dobbs, *The Janus Faces of Genius: The Role of Alchemy in Newton's Thought* (Cambridge: Cambridge University Press, 1991), 10.

34. Samuel Eliot Morison, "History as a Literary Art: An Appeal to Young Historians," *Old South Leaflets* ser. 2, no. 1 (Boston: Old South Association, 1946), 7.

35. Cicero, *Pro Publio Sestio*, 2 no. 62. As quoted by John Bartlett and Justin Kaplan, eds., *Bartlett's Familiar Quotations*, 16th ed. (Boston: Little Brown, 1992), 87.

36. These suggestions are taken from Gordon Harvey, *Writing with Sources* (Cambridge, MA: Harvard University, 1995), 27–9.

37. Cole Harris, *The Reluctant Land: Society, Space and Environment in Canada* (Vancouver: University of British Columbia Press, 2008), 16.

38. Maurice Basque, "Family and Political Culture in Pre-Conquest Acadia," in *The Conquest of Acadia, 1710*, John G. Reid, Maurice Basque, Elizabeth Mancke, Barry Moody, Geoffrey Plank, and William Wicken (Toronto: University of Toronto Press, 2004), 49.

39. Excerpted from J.R. Miller, *Lethal Legacy: Current Native Controversies in Canada* (Toronto: McClelland & Stewart, 2004), 118–9. Copyright © 2004 J.R. Miller. Reprinted by permission of McClelland & Stewart, a division of Penguin Random House Canada Limited.

40. "'The Declaration of the Reformers of the City of Toronto to their Fellow-Reformers in Upper Canada, Toronto, August 2, 1837,' The Constitution," in Colin Read and Ronald J. Stagg, eds., *The Rebellion of 1837 in Upper Canada: A Collection of Documents* (Ottawa: Carleton University Press, 1985), 60.

41. Margaret MacMillan, *Paris 1919: Six Months That Changed the World* (New York: Random House, 2001), 45.

42. Harvey, *Writing with Sources*, 21–3.

43. Colin M. Coates, "Commemorating the Woman Warrior of New France, Madeleine de Verchères, 1696–1930," in *Gender and History in Canada*, ed. Joy Parr and Mark Rosenfeld (Toronto: Copp Clark, 1996), 130.

44. Harvey, *Writing with Sources*, 13–16.

45. *The Chicago Manual of Style*, 16th ed. (Chicago: University of Chicago Press, 2010). See also Kate L. Turabian, *Student's Guide to Writing College Papers*, 4th ed., rev. by Gregory G. Colomb, Joseph M. Williams, and the University of Chicago Press editorial staff (Chicago: University of Chicago Press, 2010).

46. Jean Barman, "Taming Aboriginal Sexuality: Gender, Power, and Race in British Columbia, 1850–1900," *BC Studies*, no. 115/116 (Autumn/Winter 1997–1998): 237.

47. Ken S. Coates, P. Whitney Lackenbauer, William R. Morrison, and Greg Poelzer, *Arctic Front: Defending Canada in the Far North* (Toronto: Thomas Allen, 2008), xi. Copyright © 2008 by Coates Holroyd Consulting Ltd., P. Whitney Lackenbauer, William Morrison and Greg Poelzer by permission of Dundurn Press Limited.

48. Coates et al., *Arctic Front*, 6–7.

49. My thanks to Alice Gorton for the use of "Prostitution and Consumer Culture in late Victorian Britain" (History 248 paper, Capilano University, 2013). Note that the original included references.

50. Toby Morantz, "Plunder or Harmony? On Merging European and Native Views of Early Contact," in Germain Warkentin and Carolyn Podruchny, eds., *Decentring the Renaissance: Canada and Europe in Multidisciplinary Perspective* (Toronto: University of Toronto Press, 2001), 53.

51. William Cronon, *Changes in the Land: Indians, Colonists, and the Ecology of New England* (New York: Hill and Wang, 1983), 6.

52. Carl Degler, *In Search of Human Nature: The Decline and Revival of Darwinism in American Social Thought* (Oxford: Oxford University Press, 1991), vii.

53. Andrea Geiger, *Subverting Exclusion: Transpacific Encounters with Race, Caste, and Borders, 1885–1928* (New Haven and London: Yale University Press, 2011), 3.

54. Afua Cooper, *The Hanging of Angélique: The Untold Story of Canadian Slavery and the Burning of Old Montreal* (Toronto: HarperCollins, 2006), 14.

55. Robert S. McElvaine, *Eve's Seed: Biology, the Sexes, and the Course of History* (New York: McGraw-Hill, 2001), 26–32.

56. Mercedes Steedman, "The Red Petticoat Brigade: Mine Mill Women's Auxiliaries and the 'Threat from Within,' 1940s–70s," chapter 15 in *Whose National Security?: Canadian State Surveillance and the Creation of Enemies*, Gary Kinsman, Deter K. Buse, and Mercedes Steedman, eds., (Toronto: Between the Lines, 2000): 55–71. Reprinted by permission of Between the Lines.

57. Herodotus, *The Histories*, trans. Aubrey de Sélincourt (New York: Penguin Classics, 1954; rev. ed. 1983), 519.

58. Starr, *History of the Ancient World*, 294–5.

59. Franklin W. Knight, *The Caribbean: The Genesis of a Fragmented Nationalism*, 2nd ed. (New York: Oxford University Press, 1990).

60. Jonathan F. Vance, *Unlikely Soldiers: How Two Canadians Fought the Secret War Against Nazi Occupation* (Toronto: HarperCollins, 2008), 249–50.

61. John Demos, *The Unredeemed Captive: A Family Story from Early America* (New York: Vintage Books, 1994), 146.

62. Vance, *Unlikely Soldiers*, 5.

63. Ibid., 284.

64. Winston S. Churchill, *The Birth of Britain*, vol. 1 in *History of the English-Speaking Peoples* (New York: Dodd, Mead, and Co., 1956; Bantam, 1974), 131.

65. *Bartlett's Familiar Quotations*, 16th ed., 620.

66. James Belich, *The Victorian Interpretation of Racial Conflict: The Maori, the British, and the New Zealand Wars* (Montreal and Kingston: McGill-Queen's University Press, 1989), 20–1.

67. George Orwell, "Politics and the English Language," in *Fields of Writing*, ed. Nancy Comley et al., 4th ed. (New York: St. Martin's Press, 1994), 618.

68. Lynn Truss, *Eats, Shoots & Leaves: The Zero Tolerance Approach to Punctuation* (New York: Gotham Books, 2004), 9.

69. Mary Refling et al., postings to the H-Albion bulletin board, 8–10 July 1997. To find this reference, go to http://h-net2.msu.edu/albion and click on the link to the Scholars' Guide to WWW (H-Net). Then click on "Visit h-albion Discussion Logs by month" and follow the links to July 1997. The discussion is listed under the heading "British Wit in the House of Lords."

Index